27

CARLISLE

BRIEF GROUP
COUNSELLING

0471 978 388

WILEY SERIES
in
BRIEF THERAPY AND COUNSELLING

Editor

Windy Dryden

Brief Rational Emotive Behaviour Therapy
Windy Dryden

Brief Therapeutic Consultations
An approach to systemic counselling
Eddy Street and Jim Downey

Brief Therapy with Couples
Maria Gilbert and Diane Shmukler

Counselling Couples in Relationships
An introduction to the RELATE Approach
Christopher Butler and Victoria Joyce

Brief Therapy for Post-traumatic Stress Disorder
Traumatic incident reduction and related techniques
Stephen Bisbey and Lori Beth Bisbey

Brief Group Counselling
Integrating individual and group cognitive–behavioural approaches
Michael J. Scott and Stephen G. Stradling

Developing Self-acceptance
A brief, educational, small group approach
Windy Dryden

BRIEF GROUP COUNSELLING

Integrating individual and group cognitive–behavioural approaches

Michael J. Scott

Private Practice, Merseyside, UK

Stephen G. Stradling

Department of Psychology, University of Manchester, UK

JOHN WILEY & SONS

Chichester · New York · Weinheim · Brisbane · Singapore · Toronto

Other Wiley Editorial Offices

John Wiley & Sons, Inc., 605 Third Avenue,
New York, NY 10158-0012, USA

WILEY-VCH Verlag GmbH,
Pappelallee 3, D-69469 Weinheim, Germany

Jacaranda Wiley Ltd, 33 Park Road, Milton,
Queensland 4064, Australia

John Wiley & Sons (Asia) Pte Ltd, 2 Clementi Loop #02-01,
Jin Xing Distripark, Singapore 129809

John Wiley & Sons (Canada) Ltd, 22 Worcester Road,
Rexdale, Ontario M9W 1L1, Canada

Library of Congress Cataloging-in-Publication Data

Scott, Michael J.
    Brief group counselling : integrating individual and group
cognitive–behavioural approaches / Michael J. Scott, Stephen G.
Stradling.
        p.   cm. — (Wiley series in brief therapy and counselling)
    Includes bibliographical references and index.
    ISBN 0-471-97838-8 (pbk.)
    1. Group psychotherapy.   2. Brief psychotherapy.   3. Cognitive
therapy.   4. Group counseling.   5. Short-term counseling.
I. Stradling, Stephen G.   II. Title.   III. Series.
RC488.S35   1998
616.89'152—dc21   97–45638
                                                           CIP

British Library Cataloguing in Publication Data

A catalogue record for this book is available from the British Library

ISBN 0-471-97838-8

Typeset in 10/12pt Palatino from the author's disk by
Dorwyn Ltd, Rowlands Castle, Hants
Printed and bound in Great Britain by Bookcraft (Bath) Ltd, Midsomer Norton,
Somerset
This book is printed on acid-free paper responsibly manufactured from sustainable forestry, in which at least two trees are planted for each one used for paper production.

CONTENTS

ABOUT THE AUTHORS

Dr Mike Scott is a chartered psychologist working in private practice in Liverpool where he provides individual and group cognitive–behavioural treatments for the major emotional health disorders. He is the author of *A Cognitive–Behavioral Approach to Clients' Problems, Counselling for Posttraumatic Stress Disorder* (with Stradling) and *Developing Cognitive–Behavioural Counselling* (with Stradling and Dryden).

Dr Steve Stradling is a senior lecturer in the Department of Psychology at The University of Manchester. He is the author of *Counselling for Posttraumatic Stress Disorder* (with Scott), *Developing Cognitive–Behavioural Counselling* (with Scott and Dryden), *Dealing with Stress* (with Thompson and Murphy) and *Meeting the Stress Challenge* (with Thompson, Murphy and O'Neill).

SERIES PREFACE

In recent years, the field of counselling and psychotherapy has become preoccupied with brief forms of intervention. While some of this interest has been motivated by expediency – reducing the amount of help that is offered to clients to make the best use of diminishing resources – there has also developed the view that brief therapy may be the treatment of choice for many people seeking therapeutic help. It is with the latter view in mind that the Wiley Series in Brief Therapy and Counselling was developed.

This series of practical texts considers different forms of brief therapy and counselling as they are practised in different settings and with different client groups. While no book can substitute for vigorous training and supervision, the purpose of the books in the present series is to provide clear guides for the practice of brief therapy and counselling, which is here defined as lasting 25 sessions or less.

Windy Dryden
Series Editor

PREFACE

This book endeavours to convince the busy counsellor that small group delivery of therapy is manageable, effective, efficient and an increasingly essential part of the repertoire of the modern counsellor. Drawing together material from the first author's clinical experience and from our previous books (Scott 1989; Scott and Stradling 1992; Scott *et al.* 1995a) it applies a cognitive–behavioural framework to small-group treatment of four common emotional health problems: Generalized Anxiety Disorder (Chapter 4); Panic Disorder with Agoraphobia (Chapter 5); Posttraumatic Stress Disorder (Chapter 6); and Depression (Chapter 7).

For each problem area a 10-session group programme is described in some detail and the teaching of techniques and typical problems encountered are illustrated by use of counsellor–client interactions based upon disguised composites of actual clients. The programmes have been tested, and are recommended for use, on small groups of 5–8 persons. Whilst we believe that these programmes work best on diagnostically homogeneous groups fronted by both a group leader and a co-leader, heterogeneous groups of anxiety sufferers may be treated by utilizing designated 'core sessions' from Chapters 4 and 5, and group sessions may be delivered by a lone counsellor – though this is both technically and emotionally more taxing.

The group programmes need to be judiciously combined with individual sessions to form an integrated treatment package for each client. We recommend that initial assessment sessions are conducted on an individual basis: that individual sessions are conducted between the initial assessment and the first group session, or between the first and second group sessions, or both (typically one individual session for panic disorder, one or two for PTSD, and three for depression); that opportunities for 'emergency' individual sessions during the course of the group programme are retained; and we suggest a 20–30 minute refreshment break be scheduled at the end of each 90 minute group session to allow clients to informally raise pressing individual concerns with the group leader or co-leader.

The substantive chapters (Chapters 4–7) employ a common format. Initial assessment of the disorder is first discussed, followed by suggestions for the use of pencil-and-paper measures of symptom severity to enable auditing of the effectiveness of the programme as delivered. An appropriate metaphor for the situation of those suffering each disorder is suggested (e.g., for GAD, 'Your alarm system is set too sensitively and you are exhausted from dealing with all the false alarms') and realistic targets for a 10-session small group treatment programme are then delineated. The metaphor is intended to act as an organizing framework for the subsequent demands placed upon the clients in the typically psycho-educational pattern of handouts and homeworks utilized in cognitive–behavioural counselling for the disorder. Follow-up sessions at regular intervals across the ensuing 12 months are recommended to facilitate maintenance of treatment gains.

More general considerations concerning therapists, group therapy, and cognitive–behavioural counselling and the concatenations of these three topics are adressed in the Introduction, Chapters 1–3 and Chapter 8. Two appendices give the current diagnostic criteria for the four disorders dealt with here and summary descriptions of the personality disorders – which are known, for example, to complicate the treatment of depression (Chapter 7) – both taken from DSM IV (American Psychiatric Association 1994).

INTRODUCTION: AN OVERVIEW OF COGNITIVE–BEHAVIOURAL COUNSELLING

Cognitive–behavioural counselling is based on the everyday observation that different people respond differently to the same situation. Epictetus summed this up succinctly in the first century AD when he said 'People are disturbed not so much by events as by the views which they take of them' (Scott and Stradling 1992; Scott et al. 1995a). The essence of cognitive–behavioural counselling involves a systematic yet empathic challenging of clients' distressing interpretations. This does not involve asking clients to simply 'think positive' but to collaboratively discover a more realistic and adaptive view of their situation. The cognitive–behavioural counselling approach is psychoeducational in that clients are taught coping skills and how to modify negative automatic thoughts. It is expected that clients will practise these skills outside the counselling sessions and that their success with the assigned homework tasks will be reviewed at subsequent sessions.

Each counselling session begins with the negotiation of an agenda between client and counsellor. The material to be taught by the cognitive–behavioural counsellor will vary in content somewhat from one emotional disorder to another. Cognitive–behavioural counselling is brief compared to traditional psychotherapies – typically it is conducted via weekly sessions of 45–60 minutes over a 3–4 month period. Clients are taught coping skills and are encouraged to see improvement primarily as a consequence of their practice of those skills, not of continuing contact with the counsellor *per se*. Thus from the outset the way is paved for the termination of the counselling sessions. The key theoretical point in cognitive–behavioural counselling is that clients' thoughts and images about a situation play an important role in how they feel.

CONVEYING THE COGNITIVE–BEHAVIOURAL FRAMEWORK TO CLIENTS VIA A VIGNETTE

Probably the easiest way to introduce most clients to the cognitive–behavioural framework is via a story. To take a contemporary workplace example, consider the six employees of a large organization working in a particular unit. The organization has been downsizing for some time, and this particular unit, while adding value to the organization, might prove vulnerable. To introduce the members of the unit:

- John is the manager;
- Jean is a supervisor;
- Paul, George, Mary and Loretta are the staff members.

The job uncertainty has led Paul to take to drink. Jean, the supervisor, is feeling increasingly stressed from trying to support and reassure Mary who is very dependent – Jean is tired of the late night phone calls from Mary seeking reassurance that all will be well. George is philosophical about the whole matter, feeling that things will always sort themselves out somehow or other and Loretta has been making tentative enquiries about opportunities in another company. Both John and Jean — the two managers – feel that their situation will probably be ultimately secure but are having difficulty coping with their staff. Thus all members of the unit are in the same situation yet there are a variety of responses.

The initial reaction of people when they are asked why they behave in a particular manner is often to say 'It's just the way I am'. Indeed when Jean has been challenged by John about her excessive support for Mary she has replied 'That's the sort of person I am'. Further enquiry into Jean's history might reveal that she has always been somewhat addicted to being liked and it may well be that it was because of her popularity that John agreed to her promotion to supervisor. Jean's addiction to being liked may well have been shaped by her history.

Perhaps as a child she did not achieve a great deal but then in adolescence discovered that she could in fact be very popular and that if she was popular she could believe in and rest content with herself. Thus there are historical origins to Jean's belief that 'I must be liked all the time in every situation', and this is manifest in her current situation in which she accepts calls from Mary at all hours of the day and night and feels compelled to try and rescue her.

Paul is a 42 year old basic grade staff member. He has always been regarded as 'a plodder'. He intensely dislikes uncertainty and acts as if hassles are someone else's fault. Currently he is blaming the organization for 'Not being up front about where everything is going'. As a consequence he is increasingly taking to drink. He had joined a large organization because he thought that he would be secure there. Now that his future is not absolutely guaranteed he has withdrawn both socially and professionally. His wife has a full-time job and has said to him that even in the worst-case scenario, if he were to be made redundant, they could survive, but Paul berates himself that he ought to be providing for his wife and children 'in the manner to which they are accustomed'.

Mary was very protected as a child and has grown up with a belief that there always has to be someone strong and stable for her in order to survive. Fortunately she has a very supportive husband and has found a stalwart at work in Jean. George tries to make the most of each day, operates with the philosophy that 'You can always have a nice cup of tea', and seems largely unaffected by the uncertainty. Loretta has some concerns about the uncertainty but has been made redundant previously and had subsequently found a better job. As a precaution she is now sounding out other employment possibilities.

John, the team leader, is concerned about how to manage his unit. He is getting little clear guidance from his own more senior managers about the future and he is uncertain about how best to deal with his staff. He is particularly concerned that he is increasingly having problems at team meetings in focusing on the practical tasks for the coming week. The meetings are often, in his view, sabotaged by the anxieties of Paul and Mary. He has tried reassuring them that 'I am sure everything will be OK in the end', but he feels that this has had no effect and he has reached the point of dreading the weekly team meetings.

This illustration shows that individuals may bring their whole history to bear when they come to take a 'snapshot' of a particular situation. It is as if they focus their 'interpretation cameras' at different angles, using different mental lenses and filters. In cognitive–behavioural terms the nature of the situation is not given, each participant takes a somewhat different view. In this situation John, the manager, could do with borrowing some of the strategies in the cognitive–behavioural armamentarium.

What strategies might John use? First of all he may need to see Jean, his supervisor, and talk with her about whether she absolutely must have everyone's approval in every situation all the time and whether this is in fact practically possible. They might need to focus on the guilt feelings she may experience if, for example, she were to ask Mary not to ring her after, say, 8.00 p.m. John may have to explain to Jean that it is possible to feel guilty while not actually being guilty, that is, she should not engage in 'emotional reasoning', and that it is going to be important for her to learn to cope with these guilt feelings. John may of course already have sent Jean on an assertiveness course and she may have learnt the behaviours of being assertive in a role play, but she has difficulty in giving herself permission to be assertive because of her guilt feelings. The focus in cognitive–behavioural counselling is not only on the behaviours, such as being assertive, but also on the thought processes. For example, one might get Jean to ask herself 'Am I absolutely sure that these feelings of guilt are evidence of guilt?' John might encourage and support Jean by telling her that she will gradually get used to the small doses of guilt feelings.

Similarly Jean might be encouraged to challenge Mary's belief that she can only cope if somebody strong and stable is there for her at every turn by suggesting to her that she perform some tasks independently without seeking reassurance and see what actually happens. This strategy in cognitive–behavioural terms is called collaborative empiricism: empiricism because it involves a testing out of beliefs that are problematic, such as 'I am too weak to do anything by myself'; collaborative because the counsellor and client negotiate and agree what is to be tested and how. John would, however, have to be careful to tell Jean that she must show due empathy, warmth and positive regard for Mary if the latter is to tackle tasks by herself. If she does not display these human qualities for her, Mary will probably not engage in the tasks. In cognitive–behavioural counselling the human qualities are given the same status as the technical aspects such as testing out beliefs.

John gets frustrated at team meetings because Paul keeps homing in and dwelling on the negative aspect of every proposal John comes up with. In their work arrangements they are necessarily conducting a series of 'experiments' and are unsure whether any particular experiment will yield fruit and it is always possible to find some reason why a particular proposal might not turn out the way they would wish. John is aware that Paul can readily identify potential faults but he dwells on these faults, discouraging the whole unit from embarking on a particular project. In fact Paul is using what in cognitive–behavioural terms is called a mental filter, homing in on the negative of a situation, dwelling on it and distorting the whole. John has found Paul's use of a mental filter very off-putting. He has been unable to rationally dismiss each of Paul's objections because there is a grain of truth in what he is saying in the meetings, however, his emotional reaction is that it is a distortion. John needs to be able to call Paul's attention to the use of the mental filter and suggest that he look at each proposal as a whole, assessing the pluses as well as the minuses. The use of the mental filter is very common in clients who are depressed (see Figure 7.5) and they often cope with their depression by resorting to alcohol or drugs.

Paul and Mary's common complaint at unit meetings whenever a new project is suggested is that they doubt whether it is worth investing in because they do not know what the future holds. The other members of the group have found this very irritating because it holds up progress. Indeed George became uncharacteristically angry with Paul on one occasion because of this, which has soured relations further.

Fortunately John has just attended a cognitive–behavioural 'Managing Without Distress' day and has in mind to try out a number of different strategies. He has realized that Paul and Mary in particular are not problem orientated, it is as if they are constantly playing their personal 'horror videos' of the future, picturing themselves becoming unemployed and destitute and as a consequence of this horror video they are not engaging in solving current problems. This tendency of theirs to play horror videos in the face of adversity may be almost life long. Nevertheless John has decided that at the next meeting he will try to construct with Paul and Mary a 'reality video'. This reality video contains the most likely sequence of events – those events that a person would likely bet money on (see Figure 4.2). John begins the meeting by asking Paul and Mary what they envisage a typical day will be like in six weeks time and they are asked to conjure up a graphic and detailed description of it. The next stage in the construction of the reality video is to envisage a typical day in six months time and to detail it. Armed with the new reality video Paul and Mary are asked to remove the horror video when they feel flustered about the future and replace it with the detailed reality video. This exemplifies the cognitive–behavioural strategy that the thoughts and images of a person have a major influence on their emotional response. It should be noted that John is not attempting to simply replace the horror video with an anodyne video containing bland reassurance, but that he is challenging Paul and Mary to painstakingly construct detailed reality videos. He is then able to insist that they subsequently play these reality videos. This then gives them the space to lock on to the practical problems that presently beset the group.

Loretta probably best exemplifies coping in the group. She had played through the worst-case scenario at least once and determined an appropriate coping response, e.g. checking out alternative jobs. However, this coping strategy was not all-consuming, she had allotted a certain time of day at which to spend half an hour developing her contingency plan. The rest of the day she was focusing on her work tasks. This is similar to the cognitive–behavioural strategy used with anxiety sufferers known as 'worry time' (see Figure 4.2), getting them to contain into a fixed period of the day the time when they systematically sort out a problem, leaving themselves free for the rest of the day to address their quotidian tasks.

While at one level cognitive–behavioural counselling is about the thoughts and images of an individual, at another level it should consider their roles. For example, Jean had been performing the role of 'rescuer' with Mary, was getting exhausted by this and was in danger of seeing Mary as a 'persecutor'. Paul had overvalued a role in that his identity was completely bound up with being in employment, working at a certain status level and providing for his family. Whilst it is acceptable to value a role, overinvestment in a role can lead the person to become depressed if that role is withdrawn and ultimately, of course, all roles pass, e.g. retirement from one's job. Part of cognitive–behavioural counselling involves focusing on the roles that people have adopted and invested in and determining whether these are appropriate roles to have chosen and whether other roles and other scripts may not now be more appropriate. Thus cognitive–behavioural counselling can be conducted at the level of thoughts, images and problem solving or at the level of roles.

In some situations, e.g. bullying at work, the environment may have become so toxic that the individual has no alternative but to withdraw from that environment. The cognitive–behavioural framework fully acknowledges the power of the environment, the conditions under which people are having to operate, in determining behaviour – but for his environment Paul would probably not have resorted to drink – but the variety of response amongst the workplace team illustrates that individuals' interpretations of their environment are crucial to a full understanding of their behaviour. Whilst cognitive–behavioural coun-selling is focused on the present it does take account of how people have come to arrive at their beliefs about themselves and their personal world and it acknowledges that individuals may, because of their past, develop prejudices against themselves or against aspects of their per-sonal world that they will need to be taught how to step around in order to function adaptively in the future.

Clients of the cognitive–behavioural counsellor, given this vignette, can be asked to what extent they resemble any of the characters in the workplace, and thereby begin to appreciate the role they play in dis-tressing themselves. John, the manager in the vignette, is depicted utilising a number of cognitive–behavioural techniques, but the cognitive–behavioural counsellor uses the framework in a systematic way in order to tackle the emotional disorders of clients. This volume aims to illustrate both the general framework and the particular tech-niques of cognitive–behavioural counselling being used in group de-livery of treatment of four common emotional disorders (GAD, panic disorder with agoraphobia, PTSD, and depression).

THE LIMITATIONS OF A GROUP APPROACH

In some ways the team meetings in the workplace example parallel group cognitive–behavioural counselling for clients with emotional disorders. However, there are limits to what can be accomplished in any group. At the unit meetings, for example, it would have been inappropriate for John to focus on Paul's drink problem. This would have to be discussed privately with Paul where he might have been admonished not to drink at lunch time because that is company policy. Similarly there can be issues that arise for particular individuals who are members of a therapeutic group that would need to be addressed aside from the main meeting. Thus group counselling typically involves a judicious blend of individual and group work.

This raises the question as to what are the limits of group counselling? Group cognitive–behavioural counselling is conducted for clients with specific emotional disorders, preferably in groups that are homogeneous. If, in addition to the main emotional disorder, an individual has other difficulties that currently preclude a focus on that emotional disorder, then that is a strong argument for not including that person in a treatment group. Thus, for example, a woman who has horrendous housing difficulties may well be a candidate for a depression group, but the fact that the walls of her home are saturated, the roof leaks, and her child is becoming physically ill because of the conditions will need addressing first in order to create sufficient space to focus on the emotional distress. Historical material often plays a part in the development of depression and this should not prevent the client with depression from being part of a group. However, there may also be need for individual sessions with some of the historical material if it involves abuse of some description.

Cognitive–behavioural counselling has been applied to most of the spectrum of emotional disorders, but it is doubtful whether it would be fruitful to conduct group cognitive–behavioural counselling for, say, schizophrenic clients. While there have been considerable strides made using cognitive–behavioural counselling in helping schizophrenic clients consider whether, for example, the voices which they hear are internally generated or truly external and in teaching them how to let go of the voices they hear (Kingdon and Turkington, 1994) nevertheless such clients are often so fragile and their difficulties so idiosyncratic that they would seem to preclude a group treatment. A group treatment modality may, however, be viable with some patients with manic depression, that is patients who alternate between periods of being excessively high and severely depressed. In such a group patients can be taught the importance of compliance with medication, how to identify the early onset of 'going high' and developing a coping strategy for this. But for the overwhelming majority of clients that counsellors are likely to meet, a group intervention can be, at the least, an important component of the counselling process.

THE SPECIFICS OF COGNITIVE–BEHAVIOURAL COUNSELLING

The cognitive–behavioural counsellor takes the cognitive–behavioural framework and applies it to particular emotional disorders. The core of cognitive–behavioural counselling usually involves clients collecting data on situations that they find upsetting by completing a chart such as the Thought Record (see Figure 7.4). The first heading on the chart is the situation where the client describes in one or two sentences what they believe has happened to make them feel the way they did. The second heading is the emotions, under which the client indicates what they felt – anger, depression, etc. Most clients initially believe that it was simply the situation they were in that made them feel a particular way, rather than their interpretation of it. The counsellor's first task is to help the client become aware of their typical Automatic Thoughts in certain situations – 'What it sounds as if I said to myself to feel the way I did'. In this way the counsellor implies that it is the person's unique and idiosyncratic thought patterns that led to the distress and not the situation *per se*.

Thus the third heading on the client's Thought Record requires a listing of their automatic thoughts ('What it sounds as if I have said to myself to feel the way I did'). It is explained to clients that what they were thinking may either be at the forefront of their mind or at the edge of awareness and that they will probably need to replay the situation a number of times to access what they were saying to themselves. Thus under this third heading the client is asked to write down what their self-talk was. The fourth heading on the Thought Record is the client's rational response. In this section the client is asked to critically examine the automatic thought and determine its degree of truth or usefulness in order to produce a rational response. In the fifth section of the Thought Record the client is asked to indicate the outcome, that is what effect voicing the rational response is having on their emotional state.

The automatic thoughts of the client that cause problems will vary from emotional disorder to emotional disorder, but each emotional disorder has a number of automatic thoughts commonly associated with it. Thus, for example, many of the negative automatic thoughts of depressed patients are contained in the Dysfunctional Attitude Scale (DAS: Weissman and Beck 1978, 1979). This scale contains items such as

- if I fail at my work then I am a failure as a person;
- I am nothing if a person I love doesn't love me;

and the client is asked to indicate on a seven point scale the extent to which they agree with the forty items of the DAS. Many of the automatic thoughts that cause problems in relationships are contained in the Relationship Belief Inventory (Eidelson and Epstein 1982). The beliefs on this scale are subsumed under five subscales:

1. disagreement is destructive;
2. mind reading is expected;
3. partners cannot change;
4. sexual relations must be perfect;
5. the sexes are different.

Similarly for clients with panic disorder many of the automatic thoughts that cause difficulties for this group are contained in the Panic Disorder Questionnaire of Greenberg (1989). On this question-naire clients are asked to indicate how much they believe, for example, that panic symptoms signal a heart attack and whether they believe they are going to faint during a panic attack. Thus though the cognitive target varies from emotional disorder to emotional disorder, the method of disputation of clients' automatic attributions is the same.

Thus a counsellor might encourage clients to variously question themselves:

- Can I be absolutely sure that I am a failure as a person if I am a failure at work?
- Am I absolutely sure it is true that I am going to faint each time I have a panic attack?
- Do I really believe that my partner should know what I want before I tell them?

The core of cognitive–behavioural counselling in using the Thought Record is very much centred on the present. Sometimes, however, clients can have great difficulty in relinquishing their current negative automatic thoughts. When this is the case a more historical focus may be taken. For example a client may be taught the WILFY technique in which the client writes down what they learnt from, perhaps, a par-ticular parent 'What I Learnt From You was . . .'. Then they are asked to write down 'The way this has affected me currently is . . .' and this is followed first by a disputation 'You were wrong because . . .' and then by elaboration of an action plan for new thinking and behaviour: 'From now on I am going to . . .'. In this way the client is enabled to step around 'historical saboteurs' and lock on to more rational responses.

Whilst the core of cognitive–behavioural counselling is cognitive, the initial focus is more behavioural. This is because too direct an immediate challenging of a client's dysfunctional ways of interpreting situations produces a defensive response and the client may withdraw – from engagement with the counsellor or from treatment. An initial behavioural focus is, in any case, often an excellent way of challenging beliefs, e.g. if the client has a belief that they are unable to function at a party, rather than argue this proposition it can be suggested that they go to the party for twenty minutes and then decide whether they can indeed stand the engagement or not. Such behavioural tasks enhance the client's sense of self-efficacy, the belief that they can influence how they feel by their actions. These tasks are usually negotiated with the client at a level that the latter believes are manageable and they are gradually increased in a graded fashion.

Typically cognitive–behavioural counselling has been conducted on an individual basis and clients would see the counsellor weekly for a three month period. The first session begins with an assessment of the client's emotional difficulties and an identification of the particular emotional disorder(s) they are suffering from. Then the counsellor explains the educational nature of the programme, that the client will be taught new skills to cope with their disorder(s) and that there will also be a focus on challenging any long-standing ways of interpreting their personal world and their negative view of themselves. The cognitive–behavioural programme may be likened to 'night school classes for your nerves' with the implication that the client will acquire certain skills, endeavour to practice them, that these skills will then be reviewed and refined and that this will bring about a gradual improvement in their condition. Thus the counsellor indicates at the outset that it will be the client who does the work, the counsellor is simply there to provide the tools. This helps to avoid excessive dependence on the counsellor.

The sessions begin with a negotiated agenda drawing upon the counsellor's understanding of the cognitive–behavioural model for the particular disorder, e.g. breathing re-training for panic attacks. Time is allocated for the pressing concerns of the client as well as the technical material the counsellor wishes to cover. Very occasionally the consideration of technical matters will be suspended because of some pressing concern of the client, e.g. a close relative dying. At the end of the session the counsellor reviews and pulls together what has been covered in the session, and negotiates a homework assignment with the client.

It is important however that the counsellor checks out with the client that the latter believes that this assignment is manageable and will produce a worthwhile outcome. Thus it is not a question of the counsellor imposing the homework assignment, rather it is an agreed way forward for the client to embark on, with the client understanding its rationale. Each session begins with a negotiation of the agenda for the session, and this is then followed by a review of the homework assignment from the previous session. In this review the counsellor goes to great lengths to understand what did or did not work in the homework assignment and works to refine the thought processes and behaviours so that such a homework is more manageable in future. Then the session moves on to consideration of new material and the setting of further homework assignments.

The cognitive–behavioural counsellor inoculates the client against failure experiences by suggesting that progress will typically be two steps forward and one back and that in many ways setbacks are important learning experiences which are necessary in order subsequently to move forward. Further, it is extremely unlikely there will not be some setbacks. This is also an important cognitive–behavioural strategy to prevent full-blown relapse when the sessions are finished – because it has been explained to clients that slips are inevitable the client does not become demoralized by postcounselling slips but simply conceptualises the slip as an opportunity to learn something and develop a set of strategies that will gradually increase the duration between slips. Because relapses – or rather slips – are seen as inevitable, cognitive–behavioural counsellors typically book two or three follow-up counselling sessions in the twelve months after treatment in order to check and refine the client's coping skills. The message conveyed to clients is that the counselling will not cure them but rather that they will function well provided that they continue to use the tools they have been taught and that on occasion it is likely that they will forget to use the tool and they then have to remind themselves to implement it as soon as possible.

One of the difficulties of individual cognitive–behavioural counselling is that the client is often so closely involved in the situation that has upset them that they have difficulty seeing how they are distressing themselves. However, if they are in a group situation and somebody is similarly distressing themselves it becomes easier to understand how that particular way of distressing oneself might be changed. Because seeing how somebody else is distressing themselves is less emotionally charged, it becomes possible to think of alternative ways of looking at the situation. Thus to return to the vignette of the workplace unit, one could imagine that Paul might be able to better see how Mary was distressing herself at the unit meetings, imagining being made redundant and signing on the unemployment register and, in his attempts to help Mary with her distress, becoming aware of how he might better construct 'reality videos' for himself. Thus there can be an added value in group cognitive–behavioural counselling. In many ways group cognitive–behavioural counselling mirrors the real world in which individuals' interpretations of situations are not in fact confined uniquely to themselves but have been negotiated in some small-scale social interaction, be it within the family or in the workplace. For these reasons, the main thrust of this volume is on the appropriate integration of individual and group cognitive–behavioural counselling. Chapter 1 rehearses further the reasons why and how a balance between individual and group delivery of treatment needs to be struck.

1

BEYOND INDIVIDUAL COUNSELLING

Counsellors are predominantly involved in individual counselling. There are very good reasons for this commitment to one-to-one counselling:

- Every individual is unique and needs an approach tailored to their needs.
- Individual counselling ensures confidentiality.
- The relationship between counsellor and client provides a safe 'laboratory' in which the client can learn to interact adaptively and to overcome possible distortions generated by earlier important relationships.
- There is empirical evidence to support the efficacy of individual counselling for a wide range of problems, including those most commonly presented – anxiety and depression.

By contrast, in group counselling there are likely to be constraints on the extent to which the counsellor can tailor the session to the idiosyncrasies of each participant. The mere presence of a client in a group bears witness of their plight to other group members, even if they choose to disclose little or no personal material, and for some this may be too great a departure from confidentiality. Nevertheless, for the majority of clients a blending of individual and group counselling can provide a sufficiently individualized approach whilst appropriately respecting confidentiality. The impetus to integrate group counselling into a treatment programme derives from the ethical imperative for the counsellor to be of assistance to as many clients as possible, given the inherent limitations on their time and energy. Those who refer clients to the counsellor and are often, albeit indirectly, the counsellor's paymaster, also have an abiding concern that as many clients as possible are helped. Failure to manage client referrals efficiently may result in a withdrawal of funding.

In the last decade third-party reimbursers have increasingly stipulated that the counsellor provide no more than a fixed number of individual sessions, typically about ten. Fortunately there is evidence that significant gains can be made with some clients fairly quickly. Howard *et al.* (1986), studying the 'dose–effect curve', reviewed the effects of a wide range of individual psychotherapeutic interventions, across a large number of studies. On average, after two sessions 31 per cent of patients were markedly improved; by four sessions the proportion rose to 40 per cent; after eight sessions 50 per cent of the patients were markedly improved, reaching 75 per cent by the 26th session. Thus the more sessions patients had the higher the proportion of them that improved, but after about the tenth session there were diminishing gains from further sessions. Hayes (1995) has pointed out that the average number of sessions in many outpatient settings, even without session caps, is four to six sessions per client, as many clients default early in treatment. However, the treatment programmes developed and evaluated at research centres are set up for several times the average length of treatment. The task of the practitioner is to adopt and adapt interventions that make a difference in the actual time available and that maximize therapist efficiency.

Because of the brevity of contact with clients, providing or facilitating access to self-help material is likely to be an important function of the counsellor. But clients are more likely to comply with a self-help manual after initial instruction from a counsellor and this compliance has been found to greatly affect the benefit derived from the material (Gould and Clum 1993). The counsellor can also better ensure that the client is actually utilizing a self-help book that is targeted for their difficulty. Gould and Clum (1993) reviewed over 40 self-help studies and found self-help books to be superior to no treatment. Their meta-analysis demonstrated that some problematic behaviours, such as fears, depression and sleep disturbances, are more amenable to the self-help approach, whilst habit disturbances such as smoking, drinking and overeating were less amenable both with and without counsellor assistance.

The procedures of cognitive–behavioural counselling are so explicit that not only can they be expressed in self-help material but they also seem ideal for translation into computer-administered form. Selmi *et al.* (1990) evaluated a six-session interactive computer cognitive–behavioural treatment programme given to volunteer clients who met diagnostic criteria for depression. Clients were randomly assigned to computer-administered cognitive–behavioural treatment, to individual therapist-administered cognitive–behavioural treatment or to a waiting-list control condition. After treatment and at 2-month follow-up, both treatment groups were equally improved and both had improved significantly more than control clients. There are some difficulties in generalizing from this study in that clients were volunteer recruits and the typical client was initially only moderately depressed on the Beck Depression Inventory. Nevertheless, such programmes could become, in the future, an important component of counselling for some clients.

The cost of a group therapy session will be spread amongst the – typically – six or so participants, making it a more attractive option financially whether the client is paying themselves or is funded by a third party. As mentioned above, there is concern that group counselling may not be capable of being sufficiently tailored to the idiosyncratic needs of each individual and for this reason it is unlikely to ever wholly supplant individual counselling. Thus counsellors should see themselves not as making a stark 'either–or' choice between group and individual counselling but rather asking what combination of the two will best achieve an adequate dose of treatment at an affordable cost.

The efficiency of individual and group therapy for depression is

	Counsellor Efficiency Score
Scott and Stradling (1990) – 12 session group programme with up to 3 individual sessions initially	14.52
Scott *et al.* (1995b) – 7 session group programme plus an individual session 'If you really need it'	13.33
Williams (1992) – review of individual cognitive therapy outcome studies (total time 12.75 hours per client assuming 17 sessions at 45 minutes per session)	5.25
Nietzel *et al.* (1987) – other individual psychotherapeutic modalities, assuming 17 sessions	4.32

Figure 1.1 Counsellor Efficience for Group and Individual Delivery

contrasted in Figure 1.1. The formula used here for calculating a Counsellor Efficiency Score is simply the mean percentage change on the
Beck Depression Inventory divided by the amount of counsellor time
needed to achieve that change, per client (average per cent change per
client per hour of counsellor time).

From Figure 1.1 it may be seen that the important contrast in terms of
efficiency is not that between differing schools of individual therapy,
with ratings of 4–5 percentage points per hour, but that between the
individual and the augmented group interventions. The Scott and
Stradling (1990) study showed that group and individual treatments
for depression administered by the same therapist to comparable clien-
tele were equally effective. A similar finding has been reported by
Zettle *et al.* (1992) who compared the efficacy of 12 weekly sessions of
group cognitive therapy with the same number of individual sessions.
A study by Nezu (1986) showed that it was not simply the effect of
being in a group that reduced depressive symptoms. He assigned depressed clients to problem-solving therapy (PST – a particular form of
cognitive–behaviour therapy), problem-focused therapy (PFT –
discussion of problems with other group members) and a waiting-list-
control (WLC). Both treatment programmes were conducted over eight
90 minute sessions. PST clients had significantly lower posttreatment
depression scores than those in either the PFT or WLC groups.

White *et al.* (1992) have capitalized on the educational nature of
cognitive–behavioural therapy to treat Generalised Anxiety Disorder
(GAD) by running groups of 20 or more clients attending six 2 hour
'evening classes' for 'stress control'. Patients were told that no personal
problems were to be discussed. The results were comparable to those
found with individual cognitive–behavioural therapy and were much
less costly. Over twenty years ago Hand *et al.* (1974) found that *in vivo*
exposure for what would now be termed panic disorder with
agoraphobia was as effective in a group setting as via individual treatment. More recently Telch *et al.* (1993) examined the efficacy of an
8-week, cognitive–behavioural group treatment for panic disorder and
found almost two-thirds (63%) of clients met criteria for recovery at 6
month follow-up. These findings mirrored those from trials of individually administered cognitive–behavioural treatment. Gould *et al.*
(1995) in their meta-analysis of treatment outcomes for panic disorder
found that group cognitive–behavioural counselling was less than half
the cost of individual cognitive–behavioural counselling for the disor-

der. Moreover, group counselling with a 30 minute booster session every 3 months was, by the 6 month mark, cheaper than a prescription of the much favoured fluoxetine for this period.

The case for integrating group counselling into treatment plans is, however, not purely pragmatic. Clients experience their difficulties in a particular social context. For example a client may have succumbed to depression in part because of the absence of social support (Brown and Harris 1978) and they may not be able to contemplate any alternative 'script' for themselves in their particular situation. Group counselling can, it may be argued, better counter the sense of total isolation and suggest a wider range of roles that the individual might otherwise construct. The group situation often provides an opportunity to see in other clients the same faulty ways of processing information and over-valuing of roles (Champion and Power 1995) that led to their own difficulties. In ostensibly addressing other clients' concerns in the group context it becomes safe to consider alternative, more realistic, ways of interpreting and evaluating the data of their own experience and adopting a more flexible attitude towards roles.

2

FORMULATING A MODEL OF THE CLIENT'S DIFFICULTIES

The cornerstone of the cognitive–behavioural (CB) approach to clients' problems is that it is the individual's often idiosyncratic interpretation of a situation that plays the pivotal role in their distress, rather than the situation itself. The CB counselling framework thus necessarily adopts an individual focus. The client may be thought of as processing information somewhat like a camera and the counsellor's first task is to assess the frame from which they are taking a view of the situation, and the particular lenses and settings being used. The construction and orientation of their 'interpretation camera' will reflect both the individual's biology and their learning history.

Within a cognitive–contextual model of emotional difficulties, problems are a product of not only how clients thinks about themselves and how they process self-referent information but also how the client interacts with others and the roles they adopt and value. The cognitive–contextual model is represented in Figure 2.1.

The cognitions (thoughts and images) of an individual, which may be at varying degrees of awareness, affect the person's emotions, behaviours and physiology and each in turn affects the others. The person experiences these phenomena within a particular social context. Thus for example if a colleague does not say 'Hello' to you when you pass him along the corridor, you may think (cognition), 'He does not like me, nobody likes me.' This may then lead to your feeling tense (physiology) and subsequently avoiding attending meetings (behaviour). In your social context your non-attendance at meetings may be taken as indicating a lack of commitment to the organization by

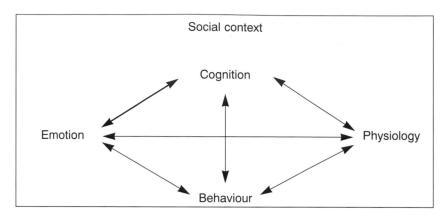

Figure 2.1 Cognitive–Contextual Model

your boss who, as a consequence, does not facilitate your promotion. If you have invested most of your energies in work – perhaps at the expense of close relationships – the emotional response may be depression. So in the cognitive–contextual model it is not only the individual's cognitions, emotions, behaviours and physiology that are important but also the goals they have, their view of their roles and of the roles that significant others play.

The model allows a variety of 'ports of entry' to alleviate distress, and for particular disorders certain avenues have been highlighted and evaluated. For example with depressed clients it may be important to modify the social context, because it has been found that both schizophrenic and depressed patients are more likely to relapse if they are in an environment where others are overly critical or involved, i.e. where significant others exhibit what have been termed high levels of expressed emotion (Hooley *et al.* 1986). By contrast, the focus in panic disorder may be on an individual's catastrophic interpretation of everyday bodily sensations (Clark and Ehlers 1993).

Cognitive–behavioural theory makes distinction between cognitive products, cognitive processes, and cognitive schemas. In the example above 'He does not like me' is a cognitive product. Cognitive products are not confined to covert verbalizations but may also include images and they share a reflex quality, often seeming to occur without conscious and deliberate effort, and for that reason they are often termed 'automatic thoughts'. Cognitive processes operate at a less manifest level and represent the mechanisms by which individuals come to formulate the judgements, evaluations, expectations and perceptions that dominate their awareness. Overgeneralization is one such cognitive process and features in the above example – 'Nobody likes me'. Cognitive schemas are the templates an individual uses to process information. They are thought to organize, integrate and direct the processing of personally relevant information. Schemas of self-referent information (self-schemas) are thought to play a central role in depression.

Despite these individualities of interpretation, commonalties have been found amongst those suffering from particular disorders. For example depressed clients have been found

(a)   to have a more negative view of themselves;
(b)   to have themes of loss compared to other disorders;
(c)   to preferentially recall information that matches their mood (Haaga *et al.* 1991).

Because disorders may be distinguished by differing cognitive content and processes, particular cognitive–behavioural treatments have been developed for each. It is important, however, to first of all be clear which disorder a client is suffering from in order to select the appropriate cognitive–behavioural remediation.

The Diagnostic and Statistical Manual (4th edition) (DSM IV) of the American Psychiatric Association (1994) uses a set of five axes to characterize emotional disorder. Axis 1 relates to emotional disorders such as depression, generalized anxiety disorder, panic disorder and post-traumatic stress disorder. The diagnostic criteria for these disorders are given in Appendix A.

The essence of assessment is to ask open-ended questions for each of the symptoms. For example in the SCID interview for major depressive disorder (Spitzer *et al.* 1990), the first symptom question is 'In the last month . . . has there been a period of time when you were feeling depressed or down most of the day nearly every day? (What was that like?) If YES: How long did it last? (As long as two weeks?).' The questions are posed in such a way as to draw out of the client whether they really are suffering a particular symptom or not. Simple yes/no responses from clients about symptoms can be very misleading and in those circumstances the counsellor must seek further elaboration as well as checking that the questioning is sufficiently open and leaves the client with enough space to explain themselves.

Each disorder has a requisite number of symptoms for the disorder to be diagnosed. From a research point of view it is extremely important to determine whether or not an individual is suffering from a disorder in order properly to evaluate how effective a treatment is for that disorder. However the counsellor is likely to be less concerned with the dichotomous question of whether a person has or does not have a disorder as with how affected they are and what is their main problem. Thus for example a counsellor may find a client only has four of the minimum five symptoms for a diagnosis of depression. This should not deter them from using the cognitive–behavioural approach to depression. Usually there is one disorder that predominates and should therefore be the main focus, but in some instances two or more disorders are equally debilitating for the client. Where there are a number of competing disorders – a not uncommon combination is depression and panic disorder – they should be given the same weighting, though historically the consensus advice has been to focus more on the depression.

Axis 2 in DSM IV contains the diagnostic criteria for personality disorders and mental retardation. The ten personality disorders are grouped into three clusters, cluster A – 'odd', cluster B – 'dramatic', and cluster C – 'anxious'. DSM IV summary descriptions of the personality disorders and examples of cognitive content are included in Appendix B. Many clients have more than one Axis II diagnosis. Even in cases where a client does not have sufficient symptoms of a particular personality disorder to merit the label, a sub-threshold level of symptoms may do much to illuminate the particular case and its treatment.

The personality disorders described in Appendix B are not thought by the authors of DSM IV to necessarily exhaust all possible personality disorder diagnoses and to cover this they have a category of 'personality disorder not otherwise specified' (PDNOS). This category is provided for two situations: first, where the individual's personality pattern meets the general criteria for a personality disorder and traits of several different personality disorders are present but the criteria for any specific personality disorder are not met; and second, where the individual's personality pattern meets the general criteria for a personality disorder, but the individual is considered to have a personality disorder that is not included in the current classification (for example, passive–aggressive personality disorder or depressive personality disorder which both featured in earlier classifications but have now been dropped). It should be noted that personality disordered clients should, according to the diagnostic criteria, have shown their pathology by early adulthood, and in the case of antisocial personality disorder some symptoms (for example, conduct disorder) must have been present before age 15.

Probably the most important issue in deciding on a personality disorder descriptor is to determine whether their current symptoms are characteristic of their long term functioning and are not limited to the current episode. Further, to be a tenable description the personality disorder should have caused significant impairment of social, occupational or personal functioning. Though there are explicit criteria for the personality disorders, agreement about whether a particular client actually meets the criteria for a specific Axis 2 disorder tends to be lower than for the Axis 1 disorders. Axis 2 provides a more fine-grained description of the client's difficulties but some caution is required in the use of this axis. For a counsellor, Axis 2 is best used to elucidate a tentative model of the client's difficulties but it may need refining in the light of subsequent treatment experience.

Physical illness may affect the course of an Axis I disorder and is recorded on Axis III. It is important for a counsellor to remember that there are many physical disorders that mimic emotional disorders in their presentation. For example, clients with thyroid problems may show symptoms that look very much like depression. Unfortunately the physical disorder is sometimes only discovered after the person has failed to respond to courses of antidepressants and counselling.

Axis IV of DSM IV is used to record any environmental or other psychosocial event or condition that might affect the diagnosis or management of a client. DSM IV suggests specifying difficulties in the following domains but acknowledges that other problems are possible:

- problems with primary support group;
- problems related to the social environment;
- educational problems;
- occupational problems;

- housing problems;
- economic problems;
- problems with access to health care services;
- problems related to interaction with the legal system/crime.

The problems listed should refer to the past year unless they have a very direct bearing on the development of the Axis I disorder.

Axis V is an overall measure of a client's occupational, psychological and social functioning on a 100-point scale which yields a GAF (Global Assessment of Functioning) score. The scale specifies symptoms and behavioural guidelines to help determine a client's score. Because of the inherent subjectivity of this scale its greatest usefulness may be in tracking changes in a client's overall level of functioning across time.

Patients with the same Axis I disorder and who have similar problems on Axis IV may particularly benefit from a group intervention, because within the group better and worse ways of handling personally relevant stressors are likely to be modelled.

There is now scarcely a disorder for which a specific cognitive–behavioural approach has not been developed and tested. Depression was the first disorder to be subjected to test by a controlled trial (Rush *et al.* 1977) and there have been more trials for this disorder than for any other. The outcome studies have shown that it is at least as effective as antidepressant medication in the short term and with a lower relapse rate (Evans *et al.* 1992); cognitive–behavioural therapy (CBT) also has a lower relapse rate than other forms of psychotherapy (Shea *et al.* 1992). The research data base for generalized anxiety disorder is not as extensive (five controlled trials) nor as impressive as for depression, but nevertheless it appears that CBT does provide short-term relief from somatic anxiety symptoms and that gains are maintained for some months (Andrews *et al.* 1994 give a review). There have also been five controlled trials of the efficacy of CBT for panic disorder (see Clark and Ehlers 1993), across which an average of 85% of clients undergoing CBT became panic free and these gains were maintained at follow-up of up to 1 year, comparing favourably to pharmacological treatments.

Research on the efficacy of psychological treatments for posttraumatic stress disorder is still in its infancy. Eight controlled studies have been conducted so far (see Otto *et al*. 1996, for a review) five of which were on Vietnam veterans. Earlier studies compared the efficacy of the explicitly behavioural strategies of flooding and desensitization with control groups, whilst more recent studies have also included a comparison with cognitive–behavioural conditions. The active behavioural and cognitive–behavioural treatments have proved superior to waiting-list control conditions. But Scott and Stradling (1997) have presented data that suggests that the flooding/desensitization procedures are often not acceptable to clients in routine practice and suggest an alternative cognitive–contextual approach which is elaborated upon in Chapter 6.

Whilst overall the CBT trials do show positive effects, they are not effective for every client and this has led to more refined conceptualizations of the disorders which in turn have suggested additional techniques that might supplement the traditional CBT approach. Some of these are also described here. It should be stressed, however, that the range of application of CBT extends far beyond the most common disorders of anxiety and depression. For example, Sharpe *et al*. (1996) recently reported a randomized controlled trial of the efficacy of CBT for chronic fatigue syndrome (CFS or ME). They found that adding CBT to the medical care of patients with CFS led to a sustained reduction in functional impairment.

Although cognitive–behavioural counselling has been shown to be an effective mode of treatment, what is achievable in routine practice is often somewhat less than the improvement reported in outcome research studies. A particular counsellor may be seeing clients with many more Axis IV problems than clients with the same disorder in an outcome study. For example, Organista *et al*. (1994) report a 58% drop-out rate in a sample of depressed patients treated using cognitive–behavioural therapy. Their US sample was low income, with two-thirds non-white, and half the total sample had a serious medical condition as well as depression. This contrasts with the 5–20 per cent drop-out rates typically reported in other outcome studies. For treatment completers in the Organista *et al*. (1994) study there were statistically significant pre- to posttreatment reductions in depression scores but not to the same extent as results generally reported in the outcome research literature. Similarly whilst Nezu (1986) has demonstrated the superiority of group problem solving therapy for depression over a support group and a waiting-list control condition, care has to be taken when generalising because the mean number of years of formal education of his clients was almost 16 years, which, in the UK, would mean that the modal client had a first (undergraduate) degree.

3

COMBINING INDIVIDUAL
AND GROUP SESSIONS

This chapter begins with the assessment of the individual, and then moves on to the difficulties that clients with particular disorders may have in accepting a group component to counselling. There follows an educational and experiential justification of a group cognitive–behavioural approach that can motivate the 'marketing' of group delivery of treatment to clients. The focus then shifts to the counsellor and the qualities required of group leaders and co-leaders. Finally practical problems in the sequencing of sessions are discussed.

INITIAL ASSESSMENT

It can sound like stating the obvious to take basic demographic details about a client but in the context of group work if there is a wide gulf between one member of the group and the rest in terms of, say, age or educational level this may lead to difficulties in integrating with the group and to the client defaulting from treatment. There is a higher risk of defaulting in a group and because of this it is important to have a contact telephone number for a client so that reasons for non-attendance can be explored.

(a) *Roles*. A counselling programme that involves both individual and group counselling needs to assess not only the client's intrapsychic functioning, such as dysfunctional attitudes and thought processes, but also their interpersonal world with a focus on the roles that they have come to adopt, invest in and are possibly trapped in. The distinction between the intrapsychic and interpersonal is often more apparent than real, in that the identities and belief systems of individuals are negotiated and sustained in small-group interactions, initially within the family and later with peers. It is thus important to determine the client's main, current life roles, whether employed or not. Perceived impairment of a main role may be a factor in depression and the inability to perform a role that has been over-invested in is also likely to be a major determinant of depression. Employment status is likely to affect the range of options open to an individual to schedule potentially uplifting events into their life.

(b) *Main problems*. Clients do not usually see themselves in terms of diagnostic labels such as 'generalized anxiety disorder', but rather as people having problems in living. It is therefore a useful starting point to ask them what they see as their main problems. In some instances the client is debilitated by the cumulative effective of hassles, no one of which would constitute 'a problem' by itself and ought, in their view, to be resolvable alone. This scenario can lead to a great deal of guilt because their situation seems insufficient explanation for their distress. In other instances the client's problems can be subsumed under headings such as finances, work, marriage, etc.

(c) *Onset of emotional difficulties*. Determining the onset of emotional difficulties can greatly clarify a working model of a client's distress. The client may present an acceptable justification for their distress which is misleading in terms of aetiology. For example, a firefighter initially explained his distress in terms of being invalided out of the Fire Service because of a cardiac problem, and indeed there had been some confusion over his medical assessments about which he was still angry. However, when asked about his emotional state in the months before the cardiac problem he admitted considerable avoidance of traumas and was terrified that he was going to let a colleague down in a crisis. In fact he was suffering from what Scott and Stradling (1992, 1994) have termed prolonged duress stress disorder (PDSD), a variant of posttraumatic stress disorder. In PDSD there is no discrete event that causes the PTSD symptoms, rather there is a whole series of traumas and the one immediately preceding the onset of symptoms may not be the most extreme. Counsellors can easily pre-judge the issue and assume that an event such as the death of the client's mother, when the client was a child, must have aetiological significance, whereas a careful taking of a history might reveal that the onset of symptoms was much later, perhaps when the child was bullied at secondary school.

(d) *Course of emotional difficulties.* If the client's difficulties are a new phenomenon then it is more likely that they will respond to counselling. It is possible to suggest to a client with a first episode of a disorder that counselling simply has to help them regain lost ground, thereby generating hope. The more chronic the disorder the more difficult it will to be to generate hope. Nevertheless, if there have been any periods of reasonable functioning, having the client attribute this to specific and explicitly better ways of coping offers the prospect that such strategies could be successfully adopted again. Clearly if the client has never functioned well then the counselling endeavour is more fraught.

In examining the course of emotional difficulties the counsellor should be looking not only for symptom patterns but also for any habitual roles adopted in relation to others. For example 'rescuer', 'victim' and 'persecutor' are common roles adopted in many client's social environments. A common scenario is that the client is given the role of rescuer at an age when they are too young to object. A parent plays the role of victim whom the child struggles valiantly (and, inevitably, impossibly) to rescue. Exhausted and protesting, the child is told that they have become a persecutor. Overcome with guilt at being a persecutor the child reverts to rescuer and so the saga continues. Distilling the script that a client is operating on opens up the possibility of a revision of the script or a refusal to play out a drama that they never chose to audition for.

(e) *Immediate precipitant for counselling.* Clients will usually have struggled with a disorder for a period before they seek help. Often they seek help when they are in too much pain and their own efforts are ineffectual but sometimes it is more at the behest of significant others. Clients driven primarily by the concerns of others are more likely to default from treatment.

(f) *Effects of previous help seeking.* Clients' experiences with any other counsellors will create certain expectations which it may be important to modify. For example a client who has been in a long-term psychodynamic group is likely to adopt a role with regard to other group members with regard to soliciting expressions of emotion which would be inappropriate in a group cognitive–behavioural programme.

(g) *Co-morbidity.* Groups should be as homogeneous as possible in terms of presenting problem. It is likely to undermine the group if there is significant co-morbidity, e.g. admitting to a depression group a depressive who also has a drink problem. To determine the extent of drinking problems in a non-threatening manner the counsellor may use the CAGE interview which consists of just the following four questions (CAGE is an acronym formed from the key features of each question):

1. 'Have you ever felt that you should *Cut down* on your drinking?'
2. 'Have people *Annoyed* you by criticizing your drinking?
3. 'Have you ever felt bad or *Guilty* about your drinking?'
4. 'Have you ever had a drink first thing in the morning to steady your nerves or get rid of a hangover (*Eye-opener*)?'

With a cut-off point of two positive answers out of the four questions, the CAGE is a useful screening instrument for drink problems but it does have a false positives rate of about 25 per cent (Mayfield *et al.* 1974).

Running a 'neurotics' group of anxious and depressed clients also tends to be counterproductive: the pure anxiety sufferers often make a rapid response compared to the depressives, demoralizing the latter. (This is not to say that mixed groups are not sometimes useful after participants have been through initially separate programmes.)

MARKETING GROUP INTERVENTIONS

There seems to be relatively little persuasion required to encourage clients with generalized anxiety disorder to attend a group programme. The group can be 'sold' as a 'stress class' and it has particular credence if it is organized as a 'night class' with assurances of 'no personal problems to be discussed' (see White *et al.* 1992). Panic disorder clients, however, typically have a higher level of associated depression than GAD clients. This means that they are more likely to engage in excessive self-blame, anticipate that they will manifest their inadequacies in a group and possibly expect that others will be critical of them. Many panic clients already fear that their symptoms mean that they are 'going crazy' and the anticipated reactions of other group members can be seen as likely to provide confirmation of this. Misgivings that panic clients have about attending a group have to be carefully elaborated and detailed counter-arguments canvassed. The temptation is for the counsellor to give bland reassurance that all will be well and to rely on his or her authority, but unless the client is taught to centrally process the various arguments they will likely default.

If the panic disorder is associated with agoraphobic avoidance then this can prevent attendance and preclude the ability to sit through a session. Group sessions are typically at a fixed time on a fixed day each week, and panic clients with agoraphobic avoidance are likely to be dependent on a key relative to bring them to a session. This can be particularly problematic if the latter are, for example, on rotating shift work. Panic clients may need reassurance that places will be available near the door and that they can escape during the session to another room if they really need to. In these circumstances it is an advantage to have a co-leader who can deal with clients too distressed to stay in the group during a session. These unfortunate events can nevertheless provide first-hand data as to how the client is utilizing skills taught to manage the panic.

Posttraumatic stress disorder clients often feel that anyone who has not been through the same sort of trauma cannot understand how they feel and for this reason a homogeneous group modality can have a certain attraction. However, they can also fear being overwhelmed if they believe that they will have to cope with other people's traumas as well as their own. Engagement of the PTSD client in a group therefore depends on emphasizing that the major foci are on lessening the sense of isolation, helping members put the incident in the overall context of their pre-trauma life, and re-connecting with the world.

Viewed from an evolutionary perspective depression may be seen as an attempt to conserve energy, not wasting it on fruitless endeavours. Many depressed clients exemplify this when they report, guiltily, that they have been avoiding friends and neighbours because they 'could not face small talk'. This withdrawal from interaction poses a particular problem when a group intervention is suggested. In addition, the depressive's negative view of themselves can lead to avoidance of people – and groups in particular – lest others discover and confirm their worthlessness. About one-half of depressed clients also have a personality disorder – most commonly avoidant or dependent personality disorder (Scott et al. 1995b). The depressed client with an avoidant personality disorder is likely to react particularly negatively to the suggestion of group sessions because they expect others to be critical and demeaning. However, the group experience offers the opportunity to disconfirm these expectations. Discussion of joining a group is a powerful way of bringing forward the hesitancies and historical origin of the avoidant personality disordered client's interpersonal difficulties. It is often these difficulties that have led to the 'hermit-like' lifestyle that has ushered in depression.

The counsellor should make it known that refusal to join a group is an option and will not lead to a severing of the therapeutic relationship. Initially the avoidant personality disordered client may be pre-contemplative about joining a group and it is pointless such a client attending just because the counsellor says that they should. The counselling task then is, *via* individual sessions, to move the client to a contemplative stage (Prochaska and DiClemente 1982) where they can see advantages and disadvantages to joining a group and have sufficient space to consider what to do. This, one hopes, will then be followed by an active decision to join. A similar approach would be used with clients with schizoid and paranoid personality disorders, though they present for counselling much more rarely. Depressed clients with a dependent personality disorder present no particular difficulty about joining a group.

EDUCATIONAL AND EXPERIENTIAL BASES FOR GROUPS

Cognitive–behavioural approaches to client's problems have the following four features, each of which lend themselves to an educational group format.

1. *Therapy begins with an elaborated, well-planned rationale.* This rationale provides the initial structure that helps the clients to acquire the belief that it is possible to control their behaviour. Essentially this means explaining that it is the interpretation and evaluation of an event that is the major influence on emotional response, rather than the event or stimulus *per se*. As each disorder is described by a particular metaphor a group modality is a particularly efficient means of conveying it.

2. *Therapy provides training in skills that the client can utilize to feel more effective in handling daily life.* Clients are asked to record between

sessions events which they experience as upsetting. They are then taught how to do a 'slow motion action replay' of each event to identify its associated maladaptive thoughts and behaviours. Finally they are taught more adaptive thoughts and behaviours. The group situation makes the transitions between the stages somewhat easier. First, clients become aware of how other clients are disturbing themselves, and because others' distress is less personally relevant it is easier to see how an alternative interpretation is possible. This cognitive flexibility typically needs development and practice with material that is not emotionally charged before it can be applied to affect-laden personal material. A premature challenge to a client's disturbing cognitions may prove overwhelming and result in disengagement.

3. *Therapy emphasizes the independent use of skills by the client outside the therapy context.* If in a counselling session the counsellor had, for example, drawn attention to a constant theme of rejection in the client's thought processes, there would be an expectation that outside therapy the client would immediately check out the rejection theme when experiencing emotional distress, and attempt a more realistic appraisal of the situation. Knowing that other group members will be conducting similar reappraisals is likely to enhance compliance with this homework assignment.

4. *Therapy should encourage the client to attribute improvement in mood to his or her own skilfulness rather than to the counsellor's endeavours.* In a group programme the counsellor is exerting a less direct effect on the client and this makes it easier for clients to attribute improvement of mood to themselves. To the extent that there is a self-attribution for improvement the counsellor will find it easier to terminate counselling.

The counsellor in individual counselling is acting as a bridge between the usually intensely private distress of the client and their engagement in a non-toxic social world. This bridge has in traditional cognitive–behavioural counselling been a largely cognitive affair involving the modification of intrapersonal beliefs and, more recently, interpersonal beliefs. A group intervention represents a slightly different sort of bridge in that in terms of the cognitive-contextual model there is also entry by the emotional port. For example, in a depression group a client may experience feeling valued by other group members, which in turn may encourage a belief that the world is not as hostile as suspected. This in turn may lead to greater engagement in their personal world. Of course in individual counselling a client may also experience being valued by the counsellor, but this may not carry concomitant action implications because the counsellor is seen somehow as 'God-like' and instead a dependent relationship is established. In this sense the group situation is a better approximation to and simulation of 'real world' relationships than individual counselling.

However, this parallel is, we believe, pushed too far when it is asserted that the group is a microcosm of real-life experience and its dynamics a mirror of what happens in the real world. It has to be borne in mind that the counselling group is an artificial construct (battering and otherwise toxic relatives, and Dickensian employers, are usually not admitted) and extreme caution has to be employed in generalizing from it to the client's social world. The first author can well remember twenty years ago arriving at a therapy group 20 minutes late because he had missed a bus and this was interpreted by the leader as aggression – 'Could you really not come on time?' Protestation that it was not intentional was greeted with quiet disdain, leading to further increasingly vehement protest, which was then taken as confirmation of aggression! There then followed an hour's silence in which the author shifted uncomfortably in his chair thinking 'What a waste of time!' – clearly further evidence of aggression! This sort of charade is, in the authors' view, unpleasant but not uncommon.

GROUP LEADER QUALITIES

There is a strong belief amongst mental health professionals that the particular characteristics of a group leader will affect outcome. Antonuccio *et al.* (1982) examined the characteristics of each of eight leaders conducting two psychoeducational treatment groups consisting of five–eight clients per group. Observers used objective rating scales to rate the leaders on the following dimensions:

1. group participation level;
2. group cohesiveness;
3. session length;
4. warmth;
5. enthusiasm;
6. clarity;
7. on-task activity;

8.   specificity of feedback;
9.   expectation of participant treatability.

There were significant differences between the leaders on all nine dimensions. Historically there has been much emphasis and effort expended on ensuring that group leaders rate optimally on the above dimensions (although the psychodynamic and humanistic schools of psychotherapy have tended to emphasize the first five or six dimensions at the expense of areas seven and eight). However, in the Antonuccio *et al.* (1982) study there were no differences between leaders in the degree of improvement achieved with clients. The therapists in this study were guided by a detailed, standard treatment manual and they participated in a 3-month didactic–experiential training programme before leading their own groups. Whilst some care has to taken in generalizing from this study (it was confined to depressed clients) it does appear that provided counsellors are experienced and competent in individual counselling and are following an approach that is manualized, additional individual differences in group leaders are of little significance.

Role of the Co-leader

The co-leader provides a complementary role to that of the leader. He or she may keep track of the various assessment devices completed by group members and highlight for the leader any changes of symptoms, e.g. a newly completed Beck Depression Inventory by a client may indicate suicidal intent. The co-leader can also review the homework assignments completed by clients and introduce them into the session where pertinent. Inevitably from time to time the group leader reaches something of an impasse in explaining a point to a group member, and the intervention of the co-leader can help to clarify matters. This also gives the leader a respite in which to take stock and review whether the group is wandering off-target.

The leader and co-leader will need a pre-session planning meeting and a post-session debriefing. Group members may have had or be having individual sessions with either the leader or co-leader. An individual practitioner is likely to have more difficulty getting sufficient clients with one disorder to make a group viable; matters are obviously easier with two involved. And acting as a co-leader is a useful stepping stone to becoming a group leader.

SEQUENCING INDIVIDUAL AND GROUP SESSIONS

An individual assessment is a necessary prelude to both individual and group counselling. The importance of complementary individual sessions varies from disorder to disorder. At one extreme there is no reason why a group intervention should not be the major modality available to generalized anxiety disordered clients. For panic disorder clients the group format can be the main therapeutic tool. But it is easier to personalize interoceptive exposure exercises for panic clients in individual sessions. Panic clients also appear more susceptible to the effects of stressful life events, e.g. a minor car crash or family row, which increases the frequency of panic attacks and can lead to severe agoraphobic avoidance. Setbacks due to crises can be more thoroughly tackled in an individual session. It is recommended that during a group programme for panic one individual session is arranged after the first group session and it is made known that 'emergency' individual sessions are available if necessary. In practice most clients have no more than one 'emergency' session per group programme. This strategy helps prevent derailment of group sessions by crises.

PTSD clients have, almost by definition, difficulty in interacting with the memory of their trauma and strenuously apply avoidance techniques not only to the place but to the recall of their trauma. But adaptive interaction with the memory of the trauma, which involves putting it in the context of their overall pre-trauma life experience, does first of all require an acknowledgement of the trauma at a primarily perceptual level – the sights, sounds, smells, etc. This acknowledgement is inherently painful, and accordingly it is again recommended that after the first group PTSD session there is an individual session before the second group session.

Olmsted et al. (1991) have suggested that for bulimic clients possibly the most efficient scenario is to have five 90 minute group-based educational sessions, with those who have not improved sufficiently subsequently offered individual cognitive–behavioural counselling. (They found that the five educational sessions were as effective as 19 individual cognitive–behavioural sessions for the healthiest 25–45 per cent of the bulimic sample). Enright (1991) has evaluated a group treatment for obsessive–compulsive disorder (OCD). Whilst specific effects on the reduction of OCD symptoms were small there were important positive non-specific effects achieved relating to enhanced mood,

reduction of the disabling effects of the symptoms and clients report-
ing increased sense of hope, understanding and control. He suggested
that the groups may have an important pre-treatment role in helping
OCD clients prior to individual therapy.

Group cognitive–behavioural approaches have been most systematically evaluated with regard to depression. In some instances the
group modality has been the only intervention (Nezu 1986; Brown and
Lewinsohn 1984; Kavanagh and Wilson 1989) whilst in others it has
been complemented by a few individual sessions (Covi *et al.* 1982; Scott
and Stradling 1990; Scott *et al.* 1995b). Kavanagh and Wilson (1989)
coped with their clients' desire for individual attention by suggesting
that a short period may be available at the end of a session but this
would obviously need to be time limited. By contrast Covi *et al.* (1982)
arranged two individual sessions before the first group session which
was then followed by a third individual session. In total their participants had 15 group sessions. Scott and Stradling (1990) arranged up to
three individual sessions interspersed amongst the initial group sessions of a twelve session programme. In a subsequent seven session
group programme Scott *et al.* (1995b) offered individual sessions on an
'If you really need it' basis. It is suggested that the Covi *et al.* (1982)
approach probably works best, as their first two individual sessions
allow clients both to form a relationship with the counsellor and to
provide the space for the client to orientate themselves to group
therapy for depression. The third individual session after the first
group session then allows for any troubleshooting with the group
modality. This particular arrangement of the individual sessions probably makes for a better 'locking-on' to the group sessions, but this
matter awaits empirical investigation.

ANXIETY DISORDERS 1: GENERALIZED ANXIETY DISORDER

The key feature of generalized anxiety disorder (GAD) is excessive worry. Many GAD clients report that they are lifelong 'worriers'. This has led to debate about whether GAD should be more properly considered a personality disorder than an emotional disorder. In practice, clients are often diagnosed as suffering from GAD by default if it has first of all been established that they are not experiencing panic attacks (a necessary but not sufficient condition for panic disorder) or some other anxiety disorder and they are not clinically depressed. The common feature amongst GAD clients is that they worry excessively over minor matters. The DSM IV diagnostic criteria for GAD are given in Appendix A.

INITIAL ASSESSMENT

The initial assessment consists of an individual interview in which patients are screened as to their suitability for a group. This interview should typically involve self-report instruments to give initial, baseline measures of the severity of a client's difficulties against which subsequent progress can be gauged. GAD clients are then provided with a suitable metaphor for understanding their difficulties which also provides a framework for locating the coping skills they are to be taught.

AUDITING THE GAD GROUP PROGRAMME

In addition to using diagnostic criteria it is important to supplement the findings of the assessment interview using self-report measures.

Such instruments also provide metrics for subsequently auditing the effectiveness of a treatment programme. For GAD clients the authors routinely use the following.

(a) *The Hospital Anxiety and Depression Scale* (Snaith and Zigmond 1983) is a brief and easily administered instrument where a score over 10 on the anxiety subscale indicates a probable 'case' of anxiety and a score over 10 on the depression subscale indicates a probable 'case' of depression. Below 8 on either subscale is taken to indicate 'normal', with the intermediate zone labelled 'borderline'. Diagnosed anxious clients typically score 14 to 16 on the anxiety subscale and between 7 and 10 on the depression subscale indicating pathological levels of anxiety and high normal or borderline levels of co-morbid depression.

(b) *The Beck Anxiety Inventory* (Beck and Steer 1990). Scott *et al.* (1995b) found that GAD clients typically score about 20 on the BAI at initial assessment, decreasing to about 13 after a group programme similar to the one described below.

(c) *The Beck Depression Inventory* (Beck *et al.* 1961). Again GAD clients typically score about 20 on the BDI, and about 14 by the end of the group programme (Scott *et al.*, 1995b).

(d) *The Client Satisfaction Questionnaire* (CSQ: Larsen *et al.* 1979) is a measure of consumer satisfaction. It is has eight items, three of which can be extracted for use as a short scale:

1. To what extent has our programme met your needs?
2. In an overall, general sense, how satisfied are you with the service you received?
3. If you were to seek help again, would you come back to our programme?

Each of the items is answered on a 4-point scale. The CSQ also invites clients to 'Write any comments you have about the programme in the space below'. This is a very useful way of obtaining feedback about a programme that you have run.

White *et al.* (1992) used the State-Trait Anxiety Inventory (STAI: Spielberger *et al.*, 1970) as one of their main measures to evaluate a group programme for GAD. On the State scale clients typically scored

55 at assessment and 41 after the programme, whilst on the Trait scale they typically scored 58 initially and 50 at the end of the group sessions. White *et al.* also sought feedback about the materials they used and the programme itself using the following questions:

1. How appropriate is the booklet in explaining stress?
2. How well does the booklet explain your own problem?
3. How sensible does the treatment seem to you? and
4. How well do you think this therapy will work for you?

Each item was rated on a scale from 1 to 12.

CONVEYING THE METAPHOR

The dominant mode of communication of the most influential political and religious leaders is one of metaphor or story telling (e.g. 'Jesus refused to speak to them except in parables'), and their goal is a cognitive one – to effect a change in the person's beliefs. Metaphor has been held to be a more persuasive way of communicating a message than a scientific explanation. However, cognitive–behavioural approaches to behaviour problems have their roots in a scientific paradigm with an emphasis on empirical evaluation. Consequently in explaining a client's disorder to them the counsellor is likely to attempt a scientific explanation in much the same way that medics would. Unfortunately this does not readily engage many clients because it is, to them, complicated and descriptive rather than simple and prescriptive.

The biological explanations for GAD that are usually given are extensions of the normal stress response. Most studies show that healthy people under stress show evidence of increased arousal, including increased heart rate, blood pressure, respiration and muscle tension. (For a biological explanation of the stress response see Palmer and Dryden 1995, pp. 9–11). Currently, groups for generalized anxiety disordered clients are often marketed as 'stress control' or 'stress management', and the term 'stress' has itself become a convenient metaphor. It is more acceptable and less stigmatizing to be invited to join a 'stress class' than a group for patients with generalized anxiety disorder.

The most common model of stress is a transactional one, that is stress is not a property of the individual or of the environment but a function of the 'fit' between the two. This means that the 'stressed' individual is not automatically targeted for change or seen as weak but that the environment – the conditions under which people have to operate – should also come under consideration for change.

These distinctions are represented in the 'Balance' model of stress shown in Figure 4.1 (adapted from Stradling and Thompson, 1997). When perceived demands (stressors) are out of balance with perceived resources (coping styles; formal and informal support) the individual feels stressed. In the context of occupational stress, for example, employers should modify the demands upon stressed individuals – changing the conditions under which they operate. And when individual repair work is needed, counsellors should provide support, assist clients to develop and deploy appropriate coping skills, and, where necessary, help clients to adjust their interpretation of their situation following Epictetus' dictum: 'People are disturbed not so much by events as by the views which they take of them'.

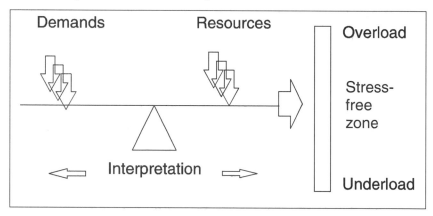

Figure 4.1   The Balance Model of Stress

The group cognitive–behavioural programmes described in this volume are as much about helping a client construct a different story about themselves and their world as with making changes in information processing. A narrative style fits in easily with a group format and is perhaps less remote from everyday exchange.

For GAD clients, 'alarm' and 'video recorder' are two very useful metaphors. At the individual assessment session the counsellor might give an explanation along the following lines.

Group Leader. With GAD it seems that the 'alarm' in your nervous system has been set very sensitively for a long time. It is as if your car had been repeatedly broken into and you have now set the alarm very sensitively to try and stop it happening again. The trouble is it keeps going off whenever a heavy lorry goes down the road and you are exhausted having to keep going out and switching it off. You are tired from dealing with all the 'false alarms'.

Importantly this metaphor implies that the anxiety relates more to past than current threats whilst acknowledging and legitimizing the fatigue it causes.

The second metaphor offers an explanation for and implies a way of dealing with apprehensive expectation.

Leader: Often without realizing it you play 'horror movies' of forthcoming events and so get yourself into a state. We don't exactly want you to play *Sound of Music* all the time, but we do want you to get into playing more realistic and statistically more likely videos of the future.

One problem with using the synonym of a 'stress class' for GAD clients is that sources of referral tend to send what they perceive as 'stress cases'. A significant minority of these 'stress cases' are in fact what DSM IV describes as adjustment disorder, that is:

(a) They do not actually meet full criteria for anxiety or depression, though there are some symptoms.
(b) A stressor has occurred, e.g. break up of a relationship or loss of a job, and the client's response either exceeds what would normally be expected from such a stressor or materially impairs work or social functioning.

For a diagnosis of adjustment disorder the client's symptoms have to be manifested within three months of the stressor and must not last longer than six months after the end of the stressor. Of course, if the stressor is one that will be continuing (such as chronic illness), it may take a very long time for the client to adjust. Adjustment disorder cases seem to benefit most from five or six individual sessions of problem solving, and the problem-solving component of the GAD programme described here (Sessions Two and Three) provides the basis for these sessions. The adjustment disorder diagnosis should be seen, however, as a last resort and where there is any doubt GAD may be assumed. It should be noted that the stressor for adjustment disorder must not be of life threatening proportions. If it were, then consideration would be given to posttraumatic stress disorder as a better descriptor.

TARGETS

One of the virtues of these metaphors is that they focus both client and counsellor on discrete targets. In the case of GAD the targets are to 'reset' the alarm, alter reactions to the alarm and encourage rehearsal of the statistically most likely sequences of events.

SETTING FOR THE GROUP PROGRAMME

If GAD clients are to have the option of disclosing personal material in the group session it is advisable to invite no more than 8 or 9 people to the group initially. This usually results in the attendance of 5 or 6 clients at each session. With groups much larger than this participants are likely to feel inhibited about disclosure. It is also important to have seats that are comfortable – but not so comfortable that participants can fall asleep!

Participants should be informed that the groups will typically be 90 minutes in length with a refreshment break at the end in which there will be opportunity for pressing but 'too personal' issues to be discussed individually with the group leaders. It should be made clear in advance that attendance at this refreshment break is not compulsory and that it will last no more than 20–30 minutes. This period can also be used for the clients to complete any self-report measures, and gives the leaders an opportunity to tease out how the session was received and to unwind to some degree. Such after-session discussions can lead to changes of emphasis at subsequent sessions. Though group programmes are often manualized this does not mean that they cannot be also tailored to some degree to the individual. The group leader and co-leader should routinely meet to review each session and to plan subsequent sessions.

It is important to stress to group members that confidentiality is crucially important if people are to feel safe participating in a group. Running a group for the patients of a particular set of GPs from whom the counsellor receives referrals can sometimes be problematic because they are drawn from a local catchment area and there is a chance that members may already know each other and decline participation. It can, however, just as often work in the opposite direction, with clients feeling encouraged that someone they know has the same problem.

As a group progresses – and particularly subsequent to the group programme – it is an asset that clients may occasionally encounter other group members at, say, the local shopping centre, and the group offers an opportunity for supportive friendships to develop. A 'local' group may result in greater transference of skills to the home setting and a better maintenance of treatment gains for participants.

However, ensuring a sufficiently homogeneous group can be a problem with a narrow referral base. It is possible to construct a seven-session group programme that meets the needs of GAD, panic disorder and some posttraumatic stress disorder clients by mixing core sessions from each of the separate programmes. This is less than ideal but the pattern of referrals and time constraints may make this the only option. The first author has found that it is viable to run such a group without a co-leader, thereby further reducing costs. However, it should be stressed that such a mixed group is not without its problems; the GAD client is typically not as depressed as the panic or PTSD client and can become fearful that they will end up as distressed and their life as circumscribed. Additionally the panic or PTSD client may be on antidepressant medication and may recommend it to a GAD client to the latter's horror. It is therefore extremely important in a mixed group to stress that though anxiety is the common bond, there are very different forms of anxiety needing somewhat different forms of treatment and that there is no necessary progression from one form to another.

FORMAT OF TEN SESSION GROUP PROGRAMME FOR GAD WITH FOLLOW-UP

Session One (Core). Introduction and Rationale

Ground rules

The opening session should begin with the group leader outlining the ground rules of the group, with regard to matters such as confidentiality, timekeeping etc., and the practicalities of the group sessions, covering matters such as arrangements for refreshment and comfort breaks, etc. It is then appropriate to present an orienting metaphor for participants, consistent with the kind of psychoeducational approach that will be followed. For example:

Leader: This is not just a group to get things off your chest, or to go over and over certain hurts from the past. It is about how you might begin to think and behave differently now so that you start to feel differently. The co-leader and I are only 'psychological driving instructors'. We will teach you new skills, but you are the ones who put them into practice. The strategies will seem simple enough but making them happen 'out on the road' is another thing. You will get better with practice, but like learning to drive a car it will be two steps forward and one back. Your practice 'out on the road' will be the homework assignments we give you each session. At the beginning of each session we will review how you got on with the homework, sort out any difficulties with it, teach something knew and ask you to apply it before the next session.

This should be followed by a brief discussion of any misgivings people might have about the underlying philosophy, though any serious misgivings should have been tackled at the preliminary individual assessment. Not to reiterate the rationale can result in members who have perhaps previously had some non-cognitive–behavioural group experience to, say, push other members to disclose painful material or to interpret another member's actions.

Distribute handout and give an overview of programme

Distribute the handout 'Managing Your Worry' (Figure 4.2) explaining that it is a summary of the action implications of all that is taught on the course and will be frequently referred to. In this first session items 1, worry time and 2, physical exercise are addressed.

The handout focuses attention on the major component of generalized anxiety disorder – excessive worry. It should then be explained that the treatment programme is primarily about removing obstacles to the implementation of the above strategies and the application of them in day-to-day life. The virtue of a brief handout is that it is a portable and succinct reference that can be used as a reminder of skills when the

MANAGING YOUR WORRY

1. USE WORRY TIME. Many people with anxiety find themselves worrying almost all of the time. Their mind may race continuously from 'What if . . . this?' to 'What if . . . that?'. They may tell themselves not to worry but they seem to worry even more. One way of tackling this excessive worry is to postpone the worries for consideration to a particular time of the day and sort them out properly (as you would do with your finances) on paper. So that when you find yourself going over and over things you shout – under your breath – 'STOP!' and tell yourself 'Now is not the time and place, I will sort that out, if it really needs sorting, in my worry half hour at 6.30 p.m. Thirty minutes worry a day is enough for anyone.' Often by the time the worry time comes around what you thought of as a worry no longer bothers you so much anyway.

2. TAKE PHYSICAL EXERCISE. Three or four periods of exercise a week for 30 minutes each time can do a great deal to relieve tension. It is the regularity of the exercise that makes the difference, not the intensity, so do not exhaust yourself.

3. PROBLEM SOLVE. Deal with only one worry at a time and form a plan of action for that worry before tackling the next one. To achieve this go through the following steps:
   (a) What is the problem, exactly? (Don't be vague!).
   (b) What are my options? Write a list of them. (Go for quantity not quality of solutions).
   (c) Write the advantages and disadvantages of each option.
   (d) Select an option (do not expect there to be a perfect solution, sometimes there is only a 'least worst' solution available).
   (e) Plan how to implement your option.
   (f) See how your chosen option works out. Most solutions are at best partial solutions and so you might have to go back to (b) and consider trying something else as well or instead.

Problem-solving is like a footballer keeping his eye on the ball, instead of getting distracted from the game of life with thoughts such as 'Have I really got what it takes?', 'It's not fair!', 'It's terrible!'. No task interfering ideas please – switch to problem-solving. But make sure that you really should be playing in this game i.e., are you absolutely sure that this is not really someone else's problem, if it is pass it back!

4. PLAY REALISTIC VIDEOS. You can think of the mind as a bit like a video recorder, how you feel depends on the videos you play. People with anxiety are addicted to playing personal 'horror videos' and these come on almost automatically, e.g. a close relative is going on holiday, and it is as if they play a video of the plane crashing, attending the funeral and then imagine Christmas without them. When you begin to feel frightened press the STOP! button on your horror video, take it out and replace it

Figure 4.2 'Managing Your Worry' Handout for GAD Clients

with a realistic video. A realistic video contains the most likely sequence of events in graphic detail. To sort out what is realistic ask yourself what would I bet £10 on happening? Then play the realistic video in great detail, e.g. 'I can see John at the airport, then going into the Duty Free, he just sleeps his way through the flight, he usually gives me a ring about an hour after his arrival at his hotel'. To change the frightened feeling you have to pay a great deal of attention to the realistic video – it is not enough to simply say 'I suppose all will be well'.

People who play catastrophe videos seek reassurance from others that all will be well, but there can never be enough of this reassurance – it is like alcohol for an alcoholic – so do not seek reassurance from friends or family, and ask them not to give it.

5. LOOK FOR ALTERNATIVE EXPLANATIONS. Look for alternative explanations for your tension rather than for some present threat or danger. Many people with anxiety report that 'If I am not worried about one thing I am worried about something else,' i.e. the content of their worries changes. The fact that they have stopped worrying about one thing and moved on to something else suggests that their particular worry could not in fact explain their tension, that is why they swapped it for another worry and why the swapping goes on and on. In fact they probably cannot justify their tension in terms of some threat in the present. The tension is most likely a relic of some past experiences – for example being frightened by a parent's behaviour or copying a parental style of making a mountain out of every molehill (catastrophizing). When you get tense, check:
  (a) that you are not catastrophizing;
  (b) whether you are absolutely sure there is a real threat in the present situation;
  (c) that you are accepting that at least some of the tension is likely connected more with past experiences. Perhaps tell yourself 'That was then, this is now', so separating the past from the present.

When you get upset do a standback assessment and ask yourself
  (a) 'What does it sound "as if" I have said to myself?'
  (b) 'What would be a more realistic way of thinking and behaving?'

Figure 4.2   *(continued)*

client is getting themselves 'in a state'. In situations of high emotional arousal a client is unlikely to be able to process material contained in a lengthy handout or booklet. Arguably, a short handout which has been frequently cognitively processed can better get a client problem-orientated, and once orientated the client should then find it easier to recall the backup material to the strategies that has been covered in the group sessions.

Clients should be encouraged to write modifications of each particular strategy for their own particular context. In the first session the leaders give a detailed elaboration of the worry time and physical exercise strategies.

Worry time and physical exercise

The worry-time strategy may be introduced by first of all explaining the futility of existing strategies.

Leader: Generalized anxiety disordered clients frequently tell them-selves not to worry and well-meaning friends and family often regu-larly repeat this. The trouble is that the more you tell yourself not to think about something the more you think about it – if I tell you not to think about pink elephants you can't help but think about them! But then you don't want to be thinking of your worry all the time. Thoughts are rather like young children, if you tell them there is a time and place for them then they will leave you alone but only if you do things with them at that certain time.

Then the worry-time strategy is read through and comments invited. The following is a typical response.

Donna. What if it is something that you just can't get off your mind, you go over and over it so that you feel your head is going to burst? (The group leaders were aware of Donna's preoccupation with whether her ex-husband might seek custody of their child despite the lack of any objective evidence that this was going to be the case. However, Donna had not yet made this information public in the group and so the co-leader responded with an example that illus-trated the principle and would be pertinent to other group mem-bers, yet would not be highly charged for her.)
Co-leader. Suppose you thought that it was likely that there were going to be some redundancies in work but didn't know how many and who. Most people would be a little anxious about this and some would be very anxious. You could have two employees with the same financial demands on them, one a little anxious and one very anxious. Part of the difference between them could be that one tells himself that he can do little about the outcome and refuses to think about it outside of the half hour when he sorts out his contingency plans, makes telephone calls to former workmates elsewhere, etc.,

whilst the other agonizes about it all day long, 'What if I have to move house? What if I can't get a job? What if the children don't like their new school? What if . . . ?' Endless 'What ifs?'.

Donna. I can't see myself just being able to put it out of my mind.

Leader. If to begin with you can do it just some of the time it gives you a bit of peace to get on with other things. Gradually you will get the hang of postponing things.

Paul. Why does it have to be a half hour?

Leader. It's just that for things that might be upsetting you lose your concentration after about 30 minutes and you start going round in circles. That is why it rarely works for couples to discuss matters for hours on end until the small hours of the morning: problems are not so much solved as one or both partners give up from exhaustion! (Laughter from the group).

Physical tension is an inevitable concomitant of GAD and can be tackled by suggesting that clients schedule in at least three periods of 30 minutes exercise a week and preferably daily. The co-leader began a discussion of what forms of exercise they could each schedule into their week and when. Two female members decided that they would both go to a line-dancing class at a local Sports Centre on Mondays, whilst Donna declared that she had no time in the week for herself to exercise. This then led to a discussion of assertion, as a balancing of personal needs against those of others, and the suggestion by the co-leader that ultimately if one did not meet one's own needs one did not have the energy to meet other people's needs. The counsellor suggested to Donna that she might try a keep-fit video after her daughter was in bed. This prompted the following exchange.

Paul. At the end of the day you are so exhausted. I used to play five-a-side football on Fridays after work but I have had to give it up with all I have had on.

Leader. Did you feel better after the football?

Paul. Oh yes, I used to go running after work as well.

Co-leader. Maybe that's the problem. At the very time when you need exercise most – when you are under pressure – it seems to slide away because it seems trivial compared to what bothers you.

Paul. Yes, I must get back to it.

Leader. People are like cars. To drive around there have to be changes of gear. Exercise is a change of gear, it is also an acknowledgement that you have rights and needs.

Over the refreshment break Paul apologized in advance that he might not be able to attend the next session because of pressure of work. It transpired that it was not that he had anything specific and unusual to tackle but a general sense of having too much to do. Mary said that she would have to leave a few minutes earlier at the next session in order to pick up her child from school. The after-session material often contains very salient topics that need to broached in an indirect manner in subsequent sessions. They are not broached directly when raised partly because of the time constraints but also because at this stage one is trying to promote group cohesion. Early in the life of a group its members are very fragile, rigidly holding to their con-structions. Then there is a grave risk that a direct challenge will alienate them, while it usually proves possible to address such mat-ters subsequently, when the sense of group membership has been established. The most ineffective cognitive–behavioural counsellor is the one who 'zaps' every negative thought the moment it comes into sight!

Sessions Two and Three. Review and Refine Worry Time, Teach Problem-Solving and Task Orientation

These sessions begin with a review of clients' successes and difficulties with the worry-time strategy. Most of the group report some success with postponing minor worries to the worry time and that by worry time most of the concerns seem less consequential. This provides an opportunity for the leader to introduce a technique that illustrates the temporary status of many problems.

Leader. When hassles or problems arrive it is worth in the first instance granting them only a 'provisional licence', because we know from using the worry time that probably most problems seem to evapo-rate. For example of a morning you might have a blazing row with one of your children about hurrying to get ready for school. You feel low afterwards thinking what a bad parent you are for yelling, that is, you see a great gap between a desired state of affairs (being a good parent) and an actual state of affairs. After a day at school the child returns home and chats amiably. The gap between desired and actual states suddenly does not seem so large, indeed you wonder whether it really is a problem at all. Of course if there were regular complaints from the school about your child being late you would obviously have to exchange the 'provisional license' for a 'full licence' and this would need sorting in the worry time using the problem-solving procedures that I will explain in a few minutes. The giving of 'full licences' first should be the exception rather than the rule. Often anxiety sufferers come from families who give 'full licences' straight away. Refusing to take the time to decide on whether to award a 'provisional' or 'full' license to a hassle or problem that has arisen means that you literally cannot 'drive' anywhere, the hassle or problem is buried – what we term cognitive avoidance – and it shows in tension. But if you continue this avoidance, blanking or blocking, after a while you may not easily be able to recall what you are tense about. Deciding on the status of a hassle or problem requires the use of traffic lights, red for stop, amber for thinking through what license to award and green for bestowing the award. If you have decided on a 'provisional licence' for a problem, changing gear by, say, physical exercise gives space for the problem to resolve.

Co-leader. It is a bit like knowing that most hassles and problems you meet will turn out to be molehills rather than mountains, so unless you have got good evidence to the contrary assume they are molehills to begin with.

Donna. But some things are mountains, they have happened and you can't change them.

Leader. That is where problem-solving comes in because there are better and worse ways of playing events, even those that would be upsetting to almost anyone.

The co-leader reviewed Item 3, Problem Solving, from the handout (Figure 4.2) then took the role of a parent who had received numerous complaints from school about her child's lateness while the leader modelled helping such a person using the problem-solving format. This was followed by discussion and then two group members took it in turn to present a 'friends' problem and to be helped by another group member using the format. As well as teaching problem-solving skills this exercise also produces group cohesion and provides an opportunity for vicarious learning. In giving feedback on the role plays the leader and co-leader ought to find something to praise first and then use the problem-solving format themselves in giving specific feedback on the less good parts of the role play, again modelling the process.

The problem-solving approach to anxiety implicitly counters the tendency of sufferers to tackle problems simultaneously rather than sequentially, but this also needs to be made explicit.

Leader. Operate a turnstile. Let through one problem at a time, schedule in enough time for that task and the inevitable interruptions, e.g. phone calls, only attempt to do a 'good enough' job (you do fewer jobs if you attempt to do them all perfectly), and have a break before letting the next problem through the turnstile.

Paul. That is all very well in theory, but I just feel so bad when things aren't done.

Leader. The length of the queue of jobs is not your problem, it depends on the resources your employers decide to devote to the task. The more you do the more the organization will ask of you. You will, however, have to decide what is at the front of the queue.

Paul. But they want everything done by yesterday.

Leader. At worst others – bosses – are allowed to change the order in the queue but you retain the right to operate a queue. If different bosses give the same urgency – the same place in the queue – to different things, leave it to them to sort out the sequencing.

Paul. Whilst I am sorting out one problem half my mind is on some other task and it gets in the way of what I am doing.

The completion of a task is facilitated to the extent that a client can remain in a problem-solving mode and continue using task-orientated cognitions (TOCs) such as 'What is my problem? What are the options? etc. . . .'. It can be explained that TOCs occur in a stream of thought. Further there may be a parallel stream of task-interfering cognitions (TICs) which usually reflect evaluative concerns e.g. 'Have I really got what it takes?', 'Am I doing well enough?' which distract from the task at hand. Clients are asked to use the mnemonic TIC/TOC to switch themselves from task interfering ideas to the more productive task oriented concerns.

Sessions Four and Five. Meta-worry, Justifying Tension and Central versus Peripheral Processing

Once again the session begins with a review and troubleshooting of the previous session's homework. Then clients are introduced to meta-worry, justifying tension and central versus peripheral processing.

Meta-worry or 'worry about worry'

Many GAD clients are aware that if they were not worrying about one thing they would be worrying about another. They already surmise that it is not so much the content of the worries themselves that is the problem but the worry process itself. Even if they are happy they worry that it is not going to last! The topic can be introduced using the following metaphor.

Leader. Worries are like a child having a temper tantrum – if you fuss over them they just get worse. Once those suffering with GAD realize they have been worrying, they often respond with thoughts such as 'Will I ever stop worrying?', 'Why can't I just be happy?', 'I have got to stop it, it's ruining my life!'. This response is like sloshing petrol on the fire, they worry even more. Does anyone say those sort of things to themselves when they catch themselves worrying?

Mary. I wonder is it anxiety? Maybe it is something that goes back years? My head just spins. During coffee after the last session instead of properly joining in the conversation I was thinking 'Am I going to be able to do this homework?' On my way here I am thinking 'Am I better?' and I get lost answering my own question, then I think 'Am I going to have a nervous breakdown?', 'What if the worrying damages me physically?'

Paul. I am exhausted just trying to keep up with all the questions!

Mary. Think how I feel!

Co-leader. All that you mentioned there Mary are meta-worries, they are nothing to do with the practicalities of making the most of today with whatever resources you have got. They are a particular type of the task-interfering cognitions – the TICs – we mentioned at the last session. You can think of them as a sort of background noise as you are having a conversation with someone. Ordinarily we carry on a conversation with someone even if the birds are singing or we hear a car pass by. If the background noise or meta-worries are grabbing your attention, imagine calmly carrying the bag of meta-worries to a merry-go-round, placing them on it, stepping off, giving them a wave the way you would a child, then feel the sensation of wading across a stream and on the other side carry on business as usual with your task-oriented cognitions – the TOCs. As you go about your tasks you will catch sight of the meta-worries on the merry-go-round. Calmly acknowledge them but do not get involved with them, i.e. do not go across the stream or climb on the roundabout. If you keep doing this you will see the meta-worries less and less often, and eventually they become a blur in the distance.

A common reaction is that a client believes that they must make strenuous efforts to eliminate the worrying thoughts because not to succeed will cause grave physical damage. This misconception can be addressed by pointing out that there is no evidence that worry *per se* damages physical health. It is more likely that a combination of worry and 'worry about worry' may have a detrimental effect.

The key task is to get group members to accept that they will sometimes slip into worrying rather like a parent having to accept that their child will have a temper tantrum and having to studiously avoid arguing with the child or in any way reinforcing the behaviour.

Justifying tension

A point not always raised by cognitive–behavioural counsellors is that a client's tension is often more to do with their past than with the present. Though the client's focus is on what might happen, the future is elaborated in such a way as to justify their current tension. Worrying can be viewed as a false justification or misattribution of tension. This can be conveyed thus.

Leader. Our bodies are very good signals as to what has happened to us in the past. Have you ever had the experience of going through an exercise programme and you have got distracted at one point, maybe started daydreaming, and you cannot remember whether you have just done a particular exercise or not? You might then notice that, say, the back of your upper arms are burning a little so you conclude that you must have done the triceps exercise even though you cannot remember doing it. Your body tells you about things from the past: you would not conclude that because your upper arms were burning it would be a really hot day when you get outside the gym. Many anxiety sufferers make just this mistake. They tell themselves that their tension is about things to come when it is much more about the past. What type of past experiences have made you so tense?

Mary. I think being adopted at aged ten. My new parents were very kind but I was not doing well in school that year, and so they sent me to another school some miles away. I missed the friends I had and I had to travel on the train by myself. Then I failed the 11 plus. I knew my adoptive parents were very disappointed. I do my best to please but I know before I start it is not going to be good enough. Sorry, I am rambling on, taking up too much time.

Donna. I wish I had your confidence to talk about the past!

Mary. Confidence?

Co-leader. Perhaps what Donna and Mary have been saying shows this big gap between how others see us and how we see ourselves. Maybe we are harder on ourselves than others are.

Leader. So long as you realize the role of past experiences in creating your tension, you can separate the 'then' from the 'now'. Some people find it helpful when they are becoming apprehensive about something to join their hands together as a way of reminding themselves that they are mixing up the past and present, then to vigorously separate them, looking at one hand and saying 'That is from then' and at the other saying 'This is from now'.

Co-leader. Maybe before the next session picture yourself as going out armed with a big butterfly net and you are trying to capture something to justify your tension, going from one thing to another. When you are getting in a state it might help to stand back from the antics of yourself 'catching butterflies' and simply smile to yourself.

Central v peripheral processing

Many clients with anxiety see themselves as having a 'butterfly' mind which races from one concern to another. This can be usefully explained to clients in terms of a continued attempt to find something to justify their tension. They stay at a level of peripheral processing of information using shortcuts or rules of thumb to an inordinate degree. If, for example, they believe that theoretically some catastrophe is possible, such as an aeroplane crash, they make it graphic and it thereby consumes attentional resources. But the peripheral processing means that there is no central anchor for their attention and they are easily distracted by the next concern. The goal is to switch them to a central level of processing in which they think through the details of a possible catastrophe and look at them in terms of statistical probability rather than allowing themselves to be engulfed in the vividness of successive imagined worst-case scenarios. The notions of central and peripheral processing can be introduced via a discussion of 'constructive pessimism'.

Leader. Some people always assume the worst, believing they should always be prepared. When things go well they can then be pleasantly surprised. They are constructive pessimists. Do we have any constructive pessimists?

Paul. When it comes to pessimism there is no beating me but I have always been that way. It drives my wife mad.

Mary. If there is a holiday coming I always think of what can go wrong.

Leader. Do they usually go wrong?

Mary. No, they are usually OK, but I get myself into such a state beforehand that I am very tempted not to bother.

Leader. That is usually the experience of the constructive pessimist. In practice the actual event works out satisfactorily usually but they have only as it were moments of relief, perhaps telling themselves 'I was lucky there' and they go very quickly on to the next thing that they have got to be pessimistic about. So in fact being a constructive pessimist does not actually work, it just leaves you constantly apprehensive and miserable. In the event of a real catastrophe happening the constructive pessimist handles it no better than the realist.

Paul. But how can you change the habits of a lifetime?

Co-leader. With great difficulty, but you can make a start by thinking through something you fear – e.g. a flight – and looking at it realistically in terms of statistical probability rather than headline pictures. Do not let your mind go dancing, think it through carefully, centrally process it rather than giving it scant attention – what we call peripheral processing. When you are getting flustered about something forthcoming you have to make a switch from peripheral to central processing. Central processing requires you to stay with something long enough to think it through properly rather than take fright and rush on to some other worry.

Leader. It may help to think of yourself as a switch, when it is up you are being a 'realist' thinking each thing right through and when the switch is down you are in constructive pessimist mode. If you are feeling low or, as in Paul's case, others are complaining about your mood, use this to tell you when you have to put the switch up to realist mode.

Donna. Just be positive?

Co-leader. No, we are not saying that, the mind knows that you are kidding yourself if you are trying to be positive. The effects of being positive do not last very long. What we are saying is to tell it how it really is.

Paul. But sometimes when you think the thing right through it's still awful! I was talking to one of my staff, we know that the Information Technology Unit is going to be cut by 75 per cent but we do not know who will go and where they might be offered posts. She was really worried and I could not honestly tell her she would have a job, at least not locally.

Leader. Often if you continue to think something out beyond the worst point, there are some aspects of it that are less than absolutely awful, silver linings as it were. In the case you mentioned Paul you might have said 'What would that mean if you were unemployed?' This acknowledges the trepidation but also helps clarify what aspect of that scenario is most disturbing. Having defined it more exactly one could use problem-solving for it. It may also be helpful to examine a typical day, say six months after the worse-case scenario has come to pass. A detailed description of the day usually highlights some positive elements, e.g. more of an opportunity for keeping fit. These silver linings can be underlined.

Paul. It reminds me of my father's phrase 'You can always have a nice cup of tea'.

The above exchange illustrates how cognitive avoidance can prevent a client seeing that even the 'awful' is usually not truly catastrophic.

Session Six and Seven (Core). Anticipatory Anxiety – Realistic and Catastrophic Videos, Response Prevention

These sessions as usual begin with a review of the previous week's homework assignments.

Mary. All week I have been worrying whether I have got it right sorting out what worries to put on the merry-go-round and what ones to postpone to the worry time. I am just a nutter.

Leader. The problem is, Mary, not the getting it right but your worrying about getting it right. This is itself a meta-worry and needs a ride on the merry-go-round too!

Mary. I am just useless.

Donna. No you are not, you are so open it's lovely.

Mary. Thanks.

Leader. Self-blame often just gets in the way of making a change. If something has not quite worked the important task is to try and work out exactly how you might play it differently. For Mary it is a case of labelling 'Have I got it right?' questions as meta-worries and taking them for a ride.

In these sessions the apprehensive expectation of GAD clients is addressed using the metaphors of realistic and catastrophic videos. These concepts are introduced by the group leader drawing the attention of group members to Item 4 on the Managing Your Worry handout (Figure 4.2) and asking which, if any, personal 'horror videos' members are addicted to.

Donna. Since the break-up of my marriage I have become convinced that somehow my daughter, Karen, who is now aged four is not going to grow up. I can't get it out of my mind. I know I am being stupid and I do not stop her doing things but it doesn't make any difference.

Co-leader. It is important not to block a catastrophic video so much as to play a very graphic detailed alternative video. Perhaps, Donna, you could imagine her on her first day at school, the tears that you would probably try to hide, then perhaps getting her first girl-guide uniform and later your reaction to her first boyfriend. Make each picture vivid so you can feel it. When you find that you are gazing at the catastrophic video awaken from your slumber and tell yourself calmly that you will watch the realistic video at a particular time later. If it is a particular catastrophic video that you play over and over it is worth having a special time for the antidote.

Leader. Some people with GAD play a catastrophic video every time they encounter a hassle. For example you have two people trying to find a flat to rent, they think that they have secured one only to find the landlord has just let it to someone else. They are both initially disappointed but one stays despondent. It is likely that this is the one who is playing the catastrophic video – 'We are never going to find a place, hunting for one is going to really get in the way of revising for our exams' – whilst the other person has a mild anxiety about the situation. The realistic video does not necessarily take anxiety away, it just keeps it manageable.

Paul. I think that is where I get in a state, I tell myself before team meetings or presentations that I have got nothing to worry about, I have done it lots of times before, I should not be feeling this way.

Leader. There is control and overcontrol. You are trying to overcontrol your feelings, Paul. It is important to accept that in anticipation of situations where, if you like, you will be 'performing', there will be some discomfort and not to apologize for it. It is unreasonable to expect to be totally anxiety-free. We need to challenge the black and white thinking of 'Either I am relaxed or I am anxious.' It is better to think in terms of moving along a line with 100 per cent anxious at one end and 0 per cent anxious at the other and the strategies you use are simply designed to edge your way down towards the re-laxed end.

Paul. What, is it more what I expect of myself in the way of feelings that is the problem than what I actually feel in stressful situations?

Co-leader. Changing your expectations in stressful situations can be an important stress-buster.

Paul. Yes, reality is easy, it is the wind up to it that I have not been able to manage.

Leader. The important task is not to let your mind go dancing by the continued watching of catastrophic videos. Many anxiety sufferers have become addicted to these videos and as with overcoming many addictions learning to overcome them involves many slips, you have to be patient with yourself whilst you learn the skill. What I want to move on to now is what keeps you hooked on catastrophic videos.

Co-leader. Usually catastrophic video addicts console themselves by seeking reassurance from friends and family that what they have just been 'watching' will not or has not happened, e.g. they ring a daughter who has just driven three miles home to check that she arrived safely, and others, usually with polite exasperation, give the reassurance. The anxiety sufferer, temporarily comforted, then sits down to 'watch' another catastrophic video and the problem goes on and on. The reassurance from others just feeds the addiction. Reassurance seeking is banned – the anxiety sufferer has instead to take on the responsibility themselves of constructing a realistic video. They, not relatives or friends, have to do the job.

Donna. It is probably why I am such a drag on friends, I keep going on at them 'What if my ex-husband gets access, what if he wants Karen to stay overnight, what if she becomes closer to him and his new whore?'

Mary. I have seen you with Karen, Donna, she thinks the world of you. It is going to be OK.

Leader. But that is just an example. Mary could spend 24 hours a day giving you that reassurance and it would not really make any difference.

Donna. She has, she has been really patient with me.

Co-leader. But it only works if you work out the realistic scenario in graphic detail, you have to centrally process it not peripherally process it by relying on reassurance.

Donna. I have got to get friends and family to be cruel to be kind.

Leader. Afraid so, there has to be response prevention, i.e. preventing the response of reassurance. After you have constructed the realistic video go and distract yourself with a task like cooking or something.

Sessions Seven and Eight. Making Emotional Arousal Manageable – Standing Back, Looking for Alternative Explanations, Challenging Maladaptive Themes, and Assertion

One of the major problems for GAD sufferers is that they are almost constantly in a state of high emotional arousal and consequently unable to effectively process personally relevant material. Thus an important treatment goal is to reduce this level of arousal so that personally relevant concerns can be centrally processed. In these sessions ways of standing back are reviewed and assertive responses are taught as a particular way of perspective taking.

Leader. Have you ever noticed how easy it is to solve friends' problems and how difficult it is to solve your own? One of the reasons for this is that people usually do not get as worked up over a friend's problem and so can think it through better. Because you can stand back from it with a friend you are better able to solve it. If we can learn to stand back from our own problems then we stand a chance of solving them. Earlier we introduced problem solving, writing down the problem on paper and going through different stages to come up with a solution. One of the reasons that works is that it stops you getting tangled in the problem, it helps you stand back from the situation. Sometimes it is not so much a problem – more a thought that is causing you to be distressed. Rather than wallow in the distress, ask yourself:

(a) 'What does it sound "as if" I have said to myself?'
(b) 'What would be a more reasonable way of thinking and behaving in this situation?'

These standback questions are Item 5 on the Managing Your Worry handout (Figure 4.2). If you can write down your answers to them this is a good way of reducing emotional arousal, though sometimes that is not practical and the distancing has to be done in your head. Could you each write down now what you think you were thinking in some recent upset? If you are unsure of what you were actually thinking at the time try and make a guess. . . . OK you have all done that, now try and come up with a more realistic way of thinking and behaving during that upset. . . . How did you get on?

Mary. A little better. I wrote down that I got upset last night at the prospect of seeing my son, John's, teachers at parents' night tonight. But now thinking it through again I've written that they have always been very nice in the past and they accept that he does have slight learning difficulties. I guess I get sad over that really and going to school reminds me of it.

Leader. That is one of the other benefits of doing the standback assessment – you sometimes find that what you thought was really bothering you is not the real problem, it is something slightly different. That other problem then becomes the focus.

Mary. That is not so bad if the other problem can be sorted, but John's learning difficulties can't.

Donna. No, but you can't help but laugh with John, he brings more joy to people than most other people I know.

Co-leader. That is what we mean by a standback assessment. Donna's just come at the thinking about John from a whole new angle. I am sure it does not take away the sadness but it maybe makes going to the school more manageable.

Mary. I know, thanks.

Paul. I wrote down my feelings of upset when a colleague got annoyed with me for making some grammatical changes to a report that he had written, but I could not think of another way of thinking or behaving.

Leader. What would have happened if you did not correct it for grammar?

Paul. It would have been circulated to about eight colleagues in different departments.

Leader. What would they have said?

Paul. It would look shoddy.

Leader. Have you ever sent something through like that uncorrected?

Paul. No.

Leader. Then how do you know others would have criticised it?

Paul. I suppose it is me and my standards.

Co-leader. Often the thoughts that are distressing to anxiety sufferers have themes of competence – e.g. 'Unless I get things spot on, I am a waste of space' – or control – 'Unless I know the details of every-thing that is going on there will be a catastrophe'. What you might do, Paul, is to check out when you are getting upset whether a competence or control issue is involved. If you are into competence or control you are bound to feel overworked!

Donna. I used to work for a boss that did just what Paul did, I just wanted to tell him where to shove it!

Paul. Did you?

Donna. No, I have always been too much of a coward.

Leader. How did you cope?

Donna. Eating loads of crisps and chocolates and then going on a binge at lunch time.

Co-leader. Maybe this is a good time to move on to assertion. Many people with anxiety act as doormats. Eventually they get fed up with this, have an almighty explosion and become aggressive, then feel guilty and resolve to be a doormat for ever more. The pendulum swings from one extreme to the other. There is another way, which is to acknowledge that you have needs, others have needs, and you will try to balance them. There is a middle position on the pen-dulum. This involves a give and take in all relationships.

Donna. I was a doormat in the marriage. I can't believe how I grovelled when he came back to me after his first bout of unfaithfulness. I was with the baby all day and then I kept her out of his way when he was 'tired' after work; he didn't do anything with her.

Leader. It's that sort of situation, negotiating a give and take.

Mary. But I find that as soon as a voice is raised I go to pieces.

Co-leader. If that is the case try not to explain yourself, particularly with people who have a history of exploitation. Use a 'broken record' technique in which you simply repeat over and over the same re-quest like a needle stuck in the groove of a record. The more you explain yourself to some people the more ammunition you give them. They focus on a minor detail of what you are saying and enlarge on it and you lose your main message, you end up feeling that somehow the rug has been pulled from under you. To begin with the exploiters will simply make out that you are in a bad mood and possibly get even more irate because they feel that they are losing control, so be prepared – it may get worse before getting better.

Mary. But I don't like to upset people.

Leader. It is impossible to exist without inconveniencing somebody. If I am in a queue in a bank then I am probably making someone behind later than they would like to be. They have to accept that and I have to accept that the person in front of me is inconveniencing me. Inconveniencing is swings and roundabouts. But if people get disturbed by the inconvenience then that is their problem. If the person behind me chooses to fume that is up to them. Disturbance for the most part comes from how the other person is choosing to look at something. You might suggest that there is a better way of looking at the situation, but ultimately the choice of viewing angle is theirs. To go back to Mary's point, for the most part you do not upset other people, they upset themselves.

Mary. It sounds like not caring.

Co-leader. Respect and caring have to be intertwined, caring by itself can be patronizing. It is respecting that other people have choices, it gives them an adult status. You indicate your care by suggesting a 'best choice'.

Sessions Nine and Ten. Review Progress, Consolidation of Learning, Planning of Individualized Emergency Routines

An important concern of group members in the final two sessions is whether they will be able to cope after the group has ended. Many GAD clients have a generalized belief that tasks are beyond their resources (the fulcrum in Figure 4.1, their interpretation of the balance between perceived demands and perceived resources, is set off-centre until this interpretation is adjusted). Tackling the apprehensive expectation about the group ending can itself serve as a coping model. After revision and troubleshooting of the previous week's homework, the review sheet of strategies taught during the programme given in Figure 4.3 can be handed out.

Each of these coping strategies is very briefly reviewed and each group member is asked:

(a)   How useful have they found the particular strategy so far? (This is also useful data for the leaders who might, in addition, ask members to rate the utility of each technique on a 1–10 scale).

(b)   What problems have they experienced in implementation of the strategy?

COPING SKILLS FOR MANAGING WORRY

Worry time.

Physical exercise.

'Provisional licences' initially for hassles.

A turnstile for problems – one at a time (prioritize first).

Whose responsibility is the length of the queue of problems? Who decides resources?

Problem-Solve.

Switch from task-interfering thoughts (TICs) to task-orientated thoughts (TOCs).

Play and construct reality videos.

Do not volunteer to be a 'constructive pessimist'.

No seeking reassurance from others – it can only come from yourself by thinking something right the way through, i.e. centrally processing it.

Distinguish between mountains and molehills.

Do a standback assessment – 'Is there really a tiger outside the door or do I just think there is?'

Stop trying to justify your tension (it's probably more to do with the past) – put down your 'butterfly net'!

Distinguish thoughts that help you make the most of today and plan for the future from meta-worries ('worry about worry').

Put meta-worries on the merry-go-round, just give them a wave when you see them but don't get involved.

Give yourself permission to inconvenience and be inconvenienced by others, recognize that emotional disturbance is largely the responsibility of the individual and the way that he or she chooses to look at something.

Figure 4.3   Review Sheet for Coping Skills for Managing Worry

(c)   How might they refine their use of a particular strategy for future use?

Clients are asked to add their own notes to the review sheet, perhaps explaining in their own words something that they had not quite understood previously, or highlighting the relevance of the strategy to a particular situation they encounter, or how they might use the technique somewhat differently in the future. This is another way in which the material taught in the sessions is tailored to the individual, helping to ensure that treatment gains will generalize beyond the duration of the group sessions. Reviewing coping skills also helps clients to attribute any improvement to skills learnt rather than to the group *per se*, thus easing the ending of the group.

It is important to stress that slips subsequent to the group are to be expected, but that they can be prevented from becoming full-blown relapses by use of the handouts to 'nip problems in the bud'. Further, with practice, the gaps between slips will get progressively longer. It is useful to have Sessions Nine and Ten at least two weeks apart to ease separation from the group. A final assessment of the clients on the various self-report symptom measures should also take place at the last group session.

Follow-up

The provision of a follow-up session 6–12 weeks after the ending of the group further eases the ending of the group for participants. The gap to the follow-up gives the client a sufficient opportunity to practise skills learnt. At follow-up the coping skills review should again be used to address any deficits. Reassessment of the clients on the various self-report symptom measures should also take place at this session. Those clients who have not made at least a clinically significant improvement in their condition should be offered an individual appointment to reassess their difficulties. Often these clients then reveal some special difficulty that has hindered progress such as a drink problem or memories of sexual abuse. It may also become apparent that the primary problem of the client is not so much the GAD but that he or she has a personality disorder. These special concerns may then be addressed, in group or individual sessions (see Chapter 7).

A particular feature of group interventions is that friendships sometimes develop (as that between Donna and Mary) that extend beyond the life of the group. This facilitates generalization from the treatment setting and aids in the maintenance of gains. A perception of social support also acts as a buffer against the development of depression.

5

ANXIETY DISORDERS 2: PANIC DISORDER WITH AGORAPHOBIA

A panic attack involves the sudden onset of intense apprehension, fearfulness or terror often associated with feelings of impending doom. Attacks usually reach their peak within ten minutes and subside within half an hour. During these attacks, symptoms such as shortness of breath, palpitations, chest pain or discomfort, choking or smothering sensations and fear of 'going crazy' or losing control are present. The essential feature of panic disorder is the presence of recurrent, unexpected panic attacks involving at least a month of persistent concern about having another panic attack, worry about the possible implications or consequences of the panic attacks or a significant behavioural change related to the attacks. The avoidance of situations in which panic attacks have occurred or are thought likely to occur is termed agoraphobic avoidance. Agoraphobia is anxiety about being in places or situations from which escape might be difficult or embarrassing, or in which help may not be available in the event of a panic attack. The DSM IV diagnostic criteria for panic disorder with agoraphobia are set out in Appendix A.

INITIAL ASSESSMENT

The initial individual assessment interview for possible panic disorder clients must assess not only the presence of panic symptoms but also the degree of agoraphobic avoidance and depression because these can have a major effect on outcome. (The counsellor should also be alert that certain endocrine disorders, especially of the thyroid and adrenal glands, can also produce panic symptoms. It is reasonable to assume that a referring physician has taken this into account but if the counsellor makes no progress with the client it is important to check that a physical explanation has been fully explored. This obviously requires some tact, but the first author has seen some embarrassed blushes on this account.) Panic disorder can occur with varying degrees of agoraphobic avoidance from, at one extreme, the person who is effectively housebound, to the person who does not restrict their behaviour at all. The degree of agoraphobic disability has a significant bearing on panic treatment effectiveness. Williams and Falbo (1996) found that whereas 94 per cent of low agoraphobia clients were free of panic after treatment, only 52 per cent of high agoraphobia clients were panic free.

Major depressive disorder occurs frequently – in 50–65 per cent of individuals – with panic disorder. In approximately one-third of individuals with both disorders, the depression precedes the onset of panic disorder. In the remaining two-thirds, depression occurs coincident with or following the onset of the panic disorder. The more severely depressed the patient the less likely the panic treatment is to be effective. Because, overall, panic patients are more depressed than GAD patients it is better, if it is practically feasible, to run separate group programmes for panic and GAD patients, though it is viable to treat both in the same group. Core panic disorder sessions that can be integrated with core GAD sessions for a composite programme are indicated in this chapter and core GAD sessions were indicated in the previous chapter.

Historically when anxiety and depression co-exist the rule of thumb has been to target the depression. However, the authors have found it useful to target the panic disorder in a group format and suggest that those who are severely depressed are offered concurrent individual treatment for the depression. In principle, the severely depressed panic disorder patient could also attend a group programme for depression, but getting such patients to attend even one group is often a major achievement and the individual sessions aid compliance with the group treatment.

Interestingly, panic disorder clients with personality disorder tend overall to do just as well in cognitive–behavioural therapy as those without a personality disorder. Rathus et al. (1995) found that while certain personality disorder traits were associated with poorer outcome, other personality disorder traits were actually associated with an enhanced outcome!

AUDITING THE PD GROUP PROGRAMME

A prime aim of the programme is to reduce the frequency of panic attacks and this is a useful index of success for clients with panic disorder with mild or moderate agoraphobic avoidance. However, it is a problematic marker for those with severe agoraphobic avoidance, as their degree of avoidance may be keeping the frequency of panics low, and as they gain in confidence and become, literally, more outgoing during the programme they may in fact experience an increase in the frequency of panic attacks. For these clients a better marker would be their change on an instrument such as the agoraphobic subscale of the Fear Questionnaire (Marks and Mathews, 1979), on which clients rate themselves on a nine-point scale from 0 'Would Not Avoid It' to 8 'Would Always Avoid It' for the degree to which they would seek to avoid the following situations:

1.   travelling alone by bus or coach;
2.   walking alone in busy streets;
3.   going into crowded shops;
4.   going alone far from home;
5.   large open spaces.

Thus on this five-item scale the degree of agoraphobic avoidance can range from 0 to 40. Williams and Falbo (1996) found a mean score for their panic disorder clients of 18 but scores extended across the entire range from zero to forty. They also found that on average clients were moderately depressed, with a score of 24 on the Beck Depression Inventory (Beck *et al.* 1961) but with a range from 2–44.

For panic disorder clients scoring 30 or over on the BDI it is recommended that they have simultaneous individual sessions for depression. The first author's experience is that a significant minority of female severely depressed panic disorder clients have been sexually abused and this is best addressed in concurrent individual sessions, though it can be dealt with subsequently in a group for adult survivors of sexual abuse, if one is available. A focus on a client's panic attacks even when it is known that it is complicated by severe depression and, say, a history of sexual abuse, is a relatively non-threatening way of engaging clients in counselling. The inertia of the depressed client and the shame of many clients who have been sexually abused make them more difficult to engage in counselling than either GAD clients or non-complicated panic disorder with agoraphobia clients – though there can be practical difficulties in getting the severe agoraphobic avoidance client to and from the group sessions.

The Beck Anxiety Inventory (Beck and Steer 1990) is excellent for assessing changes in the intensity of panic symptoms during the course of the group programme. Clients are asked to indicate on a four-point scale (0–3) how much they have been bothered in the past week by each of twenty-one symptoms, including heart pounding or racing, feeling unsteady, fear of losing control and breathing difficulty. The Agoraphobic Cognitions Questionnaire (Chambless *et al.* 1984) provides a possible way of accessing the thoughts about unusual bodily sensations that, it is argued (Clark and Ehlers 1993), exercise a pivotal role in the development of panic disorder. Clients are asked to indicate on a five point (1–5) scale how often each of 14 thoughts occurs when they are nervous. These include 'I am going to pass out', 'I will have a heart attack', 'I will not be able to control myself', and 'I am going to have a stroke'. Clients are also asked to describe other ideas not listed and to rate them.

Completion of the BAI is, in itself, often therapeutic in that it is often the first time that clients have seen their experiences summarized on paper and it can be an enormous relief to see that they are not alone with these symptoms. The Agoraphobic Cognitions Questionnaire helps counsellor and client to refine targets for intervention.

CONVEYING THE METAPHOR

Clients with panic disorder can be helped to understand their distress using the following comparison.

Leader. Learning to manage panic attacks is rather like teaching a young child to swim. First of all you get them comfortable in the water by putting on arm bands and they soon reach the point of quite enjoying themselves. But how do you wean them off the arm bands? Usually with wails, because the child thinks 'I am only safe if I have my arm bands on.' On your next visit to the pool with him you cheat a little bit, you don't blow them up fully. You are in trouble, he has spotted it, there are tantrums, drowning him does not sound like a bad idea after all! Not only does he believe that he is only safe if he has got his arm bands on, but he also believes that they have to be as fully inflated as possible. During a panic attack people have similar safety beliefs e.g. 'I am only safe if I can get home', 'I am only safe if I get more air into my lungs', 'I am only safe if I hold on to someone or something.' They are your armbands. What we want you to do is go without your armbands. Like the child learning to swim you will be terrified to do this. What you would do with the child is get them involved in a game with you without armbands, for example seeing how long they can stand on your knees as you walk around the pool. There are more duckings which are made light of and eventually the child realizes that they are not going to drown and they give up their safety beliefs. What we shall be doing is helping you to stay in situations long enough to realize that the feared disaster, e.g. going crazy or having a heart attack, is not happening. One of the ways of helping you hang in there long enough to collect the information is to teach you a breathing routine. We will even be suggesting that on occasion you try to deliberately create your feared disaster in order to see what happens.

TARGETS

Clark and Ehler's (1993) cognitive model of panic – Figure 5.1 – describes how panic symptoms are arrived at.

The essence of the model is that it is not unusual bodily sensations *per se* that produce panic but an exaggeratedly negative interpretation of

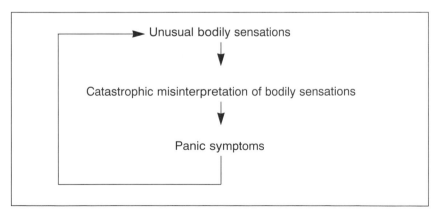

Figure 5.1   Clark and Ehler's Cognitive Model of Panic

them, for example 'This must mean that I am going to have a heart attack.' The production of panic symptoms feeds back to produce more unusual bodily sensations, which are duly catastrophized producing more panic symptoms in a circular process. Consequently much of the counselling programme to be outlined is aimed at:

(a) the testing out of catastrophic beliefs by encountering avoided places or situations long enough with the aid of breathing retraining;
(b) the challenging of catastrophic misinterpretations by cognitive disputation;
(c) increasing the tolerance of unusual sensations with interoceptive exposure.

Adapting the PD Programme for a Mainly Severely Agoraphobic Group

It is recommended that a group of 5–8 clients is recruited. Usually just one or two in a group have severe agoraphobic avoidance, and the programme to be outlined is mainly directed at such a mixed group composition. Occasionally, however, those with severe agoraphobic avoidance are in the majority in the group and the programme needs to be altered and each session extended by at least 30 minutes in which members go out from the group, assisted if necessary, to tackle a performance task. Clients with more severe agoraphobic avoidance tend to be the more depressed and need a success experience to overcome their inertia. If this success experience can be constructed for them within the group they are more likely to comply with the exposure homeworks. Having group members engage in exposure does provide life data on how they are using the techniques taught and their particular catastrophic cognitions, but it is usually not cost-effective if members are not predominantly manifesting severe agoraphobic avoidance.

SETTING FOR THE GROUP PROGRAMME

For some panic disorder clients being with other people, or being in a room with no natural daylight, or in a building which is overheated, can act as potential triggers for panic attacks. It is therefore important that the room used for the group meeting is as congenial as possible and that clients are assured beforehand that there are means of escape to places of safety, e.g. a kitchen in which to make a drink. In the group situation the cognitions that fuel escape behaviour are likely to be concerned with a perception of acting foolishly, of losing control or of being paralysed with fear. If a client does engage in a safety-seeking behaviour then these cognitions are 'hot' and can be challenged using the data from the group. Such challenges may be made by, say, the co-leader following the client to the kitchen or perhaps after the group session in the refreshment time one of the leaders instigates a challenge.

As the group progresses, members are encouraged not to escape because it nurtures a belief that had they not taken the action they did some catastrophe would have happened. It should be noted that this approach is somewhat different to traditional exposure based treatments of anxiety in which a client would be asked to remain seated until their anxiety declined. The rationale for retaining the possibility of escape derives from two studies conducted by Rach-man and colleagues and discussed by Salkovskis (1996) in which clients were told to enter the feared situation and either (a) remain until their anxiety declined (as in traditional exposure based treat-ments) or (b) leave when their anxiety rose to 70 on a 100-point subjective units of distress scale. There was some evidence that the second group showed a tendency to experience greater anxiety reduction.

FORMAT OF TEN SESSION GROUP PROGRAMME FOR PD WITH FOLLOW-UP

Session One (Core). Introduction and Rationale

Ground rules

As with all group programmes, the opening session should begin with the group leader outlining the ground rules of the group with regard to matters such as confidentiality, time-keeping, etc., and the prac-ticalities of the group sessions, covering matters such as arrangements for refreshment breaks, comfort breaks etc., before presenting an orien-tating metaphor for participants.

MANAGING PANIC ATTACKS

1. 'I AM ONLY SAFE IF . . .'. DO NOT BELIEVE IT! Hang in there by tuning in your breathing, and discover that there are no catastrophic consequences!

When you notice the first signs of panic tell yourself that you will stick around to see if the world really does end! To help you keep your cool in the meantime tune your breathing in. Your goal is 10–12 breaths a minute. Try breathing through your nose for as long as it takes to say 'One thousand' (about three seconds) and out through your mouth for as long as it takes to say 'Two thousand' (about three seconds). It is important to breathe from your stomach not your chest (your chest should be almost still), so place a hand on your stomach with your little finger over the top of your navel, and check that you are breathing from there. The idea is to strike up a nice gentle rhythm. This takes a couple of minutes for most people.

After one minute of controlled breathing just hold your breath for a count of 1 to 10 (do not take a deep breath in order to do this), then start off again, inhaling for roughly three seconds and exhaling for roughly three seconds (some people find it handy to use a watch for this). Repeat the whole procedure every minute until you have got the message that nothing awful is about to happen.

2. IN A PANIC ATTACK STAY EXACTLY WHERE YOU ARE and do not engage in any safety-seeking behaviour, e.g. holding onto someone or something, asking for help, sitting down, doing things slowly, checking your body.

3. TELL YOURSELF PANIC ATTACKS CAUSE NO PHYSICAL HARM. You are less likely to faint in a panic attack than when not having one, but you can get a 'swooning' sensation. Try and produce your worse fear, e.g. fainting in a supermarket queue, and discover that it is not actually possible no matter how hard you try!

4. PUSH YOURSELF GRADUALLY TO GO TO ANY PLACES YOU HAVE BEEN AVOIDING FOR FEAR OF PANIC ATTACKS. Spend at least 3 hours a week training in situations or places that you have been avoiding. The training should be difficult but not too difficult. You might have someone with you to help you get started in a place or situation, then have them be gradually less and less available. Plan in advance when and where you will train each week, and keep a record.

5. WHEN YOU GET ALARMED AT A PHYSICAL SYMPTOM SHOUT 'STOP!' AND SEE A TRAFFIC LIGHT ON RED. As the lights go to amber think out the most likely explanation for the symptom, e.g. breathing out of time, and challenge any alarming interpretations, e.g. 'I am having a heart attack', by asking yourself 'Would I be prepared to bet a friend fifty

Figure 5.2   Managing Panic Attacks Handout

pounds these symptoms are serious? If not then I can't really believe they are serious, they are just uncomfortable and will pass.'

6. IF A PANIC ATTACK OCCURS WHEN YOU ARE BY YOURSELF. If an attack occurs when you are by yourself try hanging in there to see that nothing happens by lying on the floor with a light book on your stomach and breathe so that the book gently rises and falls. Your chest should be almost still. After a couple of minutes you will get a nice rhythm and be able to see that there is really no catastrophe.

7. TAKE AS MUCH PHYSICAL EXERCISE AS YOU CAN. Physical exercise increases tolerance for unusual but not abnormal bodily sensations. One of the reasons for panic attacks is often a confusion between unusual and abnormal bodily symptoms.

Figure 5.2 *(continued)*

Distribute handout and give an overview of programme

The Managing Panic Attacks handout (Figure 5.2) provides a concise summary of coping strategies taught in the programme and a handy reference afterwards. The group leader should run through it with the group suggesting that, at this stage, it simply gives a flavour of the sort of strategies that will be dealt with. It is insufficient to rely on verbal instruction alone. As they go through the programme clients are encouraged to write on the handout their own further explanations of points and add on any extra material from the sessions that is particularly relevant to them. In this way the group material is tailored to the individual.

It is explained that in this first session Items (1) and (2) from the Handout are covered, but before covering these items it is important to collect information on the frequency, intensity, duration and functional impairment caused by the panic attacks for each participant.

Distribute Panic Monitoring Form and discuss

The Panic Monitoring Form shown in Figure 5.3 is introduced.

The group leader first of all explains the rationale behind each heading on the form. The first point to emphasize is that it is extremely unlikely that members will recover completely from panic disorder after their first attempts with the strategies taught in the programme. The more

MONITORING PANIC ATTACKS

Date .... / .... / ....

Time panic began ....
Time panic ended (i.e., symptoms became manageable) ....

Situation ....

Thoughts during the attack ....

How severe was the panic? (0–10: higher score means worse)   .... / 10

Did the attack stop you doing anything?   Yes ....   No ....

If the answer is 'Yes', what was it? ....

Please indicate any safety-seeking behaviour ....

Figure 5.3   Panic Monitoring Form

typical scenario is that a group member probably has four or five panic attacks a week at the start, and within two or three sessions this reduces to two or three. Recording the dates when panics occur charts the progress made. Without a record, clients are inclined to respond to the vividness of the memory of the most recent panic attack when gauging progress, and deny improvement. Making clients aware of the relatively short duration of panic attacks (usually 5 to 30 minutes) by recording them can make it easier to endure them. It is useful to compare them with the length of time that one would typically be in the dentist, an unpleasant experience but one that most people put up with because of its brevity.

Each panic disorder client will have some situations that always produce a panic, perhaps travelling to town alone, other situations that predispose them to a panic, such as sometimes having a panic attack in a queue, and uncued panics, for example when asleep. Clients can find it easy to comprehend a panic attack as a stress response, say after an argument, but find them more alarming when they occur 'out of the blue'. In asking clients to record the situations in which panics occur it is important to indicate that they are as likely to be uncued as cued. As clients progress they will also notice some variation in the intensity of distress during panic, typically after about the fourth session a client may be experiencing one very bad panic attack a week, and perhaps two less intense ones rated at 6 or 7 on the 10-point scale. Thus the record of the form also implicitly challenges the panic disordered client's typically black-and-white thinking – 'All panic attacks are awful', 'I am either having panic attacks or not', 'I am either cured or not'.

The thoughts that occur during a panic attack can often appear bizarre afterwards. Nevertheless they are believed at the time and usually lead to some safety behaviour such as holding on to something. Clients are asked to indicate the thoughts that occur even if they seem 'weird'. Collecting such thoughts leads to a distillation of the fundamental maladaptive beliefs that come onstream during a panic. Then clients are asked to indicate the functional impairment caused by the panic attack, e.g. 'I stopped shopping and went home', 'I went outside to get some air.' Finally, the form asks clients to indicate any safety-seeking behaviour, which should record not only escaping from the situation but also in-situation behaviours like sitting still or looking for an escape route.

To ensure that clients understand the use of the form they are asked to recall a recent panic attack and detail it on the form. (*Note*: it is safer to ask for a recent panic attack rather than the last attack, this gives the client the option of indicating a less than overwhelming panic if the description of such panics itself triggers a panic. At this early stage in the programme the primary concern is to engage the client and make them feel safe). The data on the Monitoring Form is then used to illustrate the cognitive model of panic.

The Cognitive Model of Panic

After checking that all group members have satisfactorily completed their form, one of the leaders asks if anyone could volunteer what they have written. The leader then uses this material to explicate the cognitive model.

John. Well, I have put down last week when I went to the barbers to have my hair cut. After about five minutes in the chair my heart was racing and I wanted to escape.

Leader. Did you?

John. No, but only because I would have looked stupid with half a haircut!

Leader. You mentioned that your heart was racing, did you notice anything else?

John. I was sweating.

Co-leader. OK, we will use John's experience to show how panic builds up by drawing it. The first thing John notices is that he is sweating and his heart is racing, and I have put those symptoms in the first column (see Figure 5.4). In the third column I have put that he was anxious, were there any emotions other than anxiety?

John. Embarrassment. I have known the barber for 20 years, he is a really nice bloke. It's stupid.

Co-leader. OK, I will add in embarrassment. So far I have only filled in the first and third columns. This is because your heart racing and sweating do not automatically cause anxiety or embarrassment, for example after exercising. It is what we think about what we feel that can lead to distress. Column 2 is so important that I have put it in a different colour. What thoughts did you write down, John?

John. I am going to make a show of myself.

Co-leader. So we have the sequence 1 → 2 → 3 on the diagram.

Leader. What effect did getting anxious and embarrassed have on your heart and on your sweating?

John. Made them both worse I guess.

Co-leader. So, if we enter this in the physical discomfort column. What did you feel in response to an increase in physical symptoms?

John. Very distressed, I just wanted to escape.

Leader. What do you think you were thinking to produce such distress?

John. I am not sure.

Co-leader. Sometimes we know exactly what we are thinking and at other times it is much less clear and you have to do some digging around to see 'what it sounds as if you have said to yourself'.

John. I suppose as I wanted to escape and could not, I must have thought that I was trapped.

Figure 5.4 tabulates the unusual physical sensations, thoughts, and emotions and behaviours of John's panic attack. A main feature of the programme is teaching how to break the chain by challenging the thoughts. In addition, one unusual physical reaction tends to trigger others, for example a racing of the heart producing a choking or

Unusual physical sensations	Thoughts	Emotions and behaviours
1. Heart racing, sweating	2. I am going to make a show of myself	3. Anxious, embarrassed
4. Faster heartbeat, more sweating	5. I am trapped	6. Very distressed

Figure 5.4   John's Panic

breathing difficulty. The modification of the physiological reaction is another target in the circular chain reaction.

Breathing retraining

The purpose of breathing retraining is to help clients remain calm enough during a panic not to engage in any safety-seeking behaviour and endure it until it becomes apparent that the feared disaster is not going to happen. The first step is to ask the group to count their number of breaths per minute. An inhalation and an exhalation are counted as one breath. Participants are asked not to alter their breathing in any way for this exercise as the goal is to establish their normal (non-panic) rate of breathing. The normal rate of breathing is typically ten to twelve breaths a minute, and this frequency serves as a 'ball park figure' to aim for in the event of a panic. Usually at least one or two group members report a frequency greater than this, and the exercise serves as a reminder to slow breathing down. The thought of this can, however, evoke anxiety.

Sara. I am choking anyway in my panics, I have got to get more air in, not less!
Co-leader. Have you ever tried not to take more air in during a panic?
Sara. No.
Co-leader. Test out what happens if you do not try taking more air in.
Sara. I'd die.
Co-leader. You would actually die?
Sara. Well not exactly, but I would be in such a state.
Stan. (producing a bottle of water from his pocket and taking a drink) It's frightening, the panic is bad enough without making it worse.
Leader. But can you be sure it would make it worse if you haven't tried it?

Stan. Well no, but . . .

John. Is that what you do Stan, take a drink of vodka?

Stan. (Laughing) That's not a bad idea, my mouth gets so dry. I had forgotten my bottle when I went for the interview for this Course, and you (looking at the leader) were running very late. I couldn't sit in the waiting room, I had to get some air outside.

Co-leader. One of the important parts of this programme is to get people to think again about their safety-seeking beliefs. Stan and Sara have mentioned three already. (Leader gets up and writes on whiteboard 'I am only safe if I breathe quickly', 'I have to have a drink (vodka, water) to get by', 'I have to go out and get air.') Does anybody have any others?

John. 'I am only safe if I am with someone else.'

Sara. 'I am only safe if I am driving the car.'

Leader. These beliefs can seem so right at the time, in a panic we want you to ask yourself, to begin with, simply 'Can I be absolutely sure my safety belief is right?' This then gives you, literally, a 'breather' to start tuning your breathing in. This question helps you to refocus.

The group leader again reads through Item (1) on the Managing Panic Attacks Handout (Figure 5.2) and answers any questions.

Stan. I never have got into a rhythm with anything, this is going to be tough.

Leader. Everyone will have a slightly different natural rhythm, it will not be breathing in for exactly 3 seconds and out for 3 seconds, that is just a rough guide. Getting the right pace for you will take a bit of practice. Perhaps we could spend about five minutes now using the breathing routine, if you can start now.

Leader. (after 5 minutes) How did people find that?

Sara. I felt more nervy to begin with but near the end I was getting quite relaxed.

Stan. It was the same for me.

Co-leader. In this artificial situation here it can be worse to begin with because you might be thinking 'I have got to get it right, what will people think?' But it is also likely to be worse to begin with during a panic because you tell yourself you have got to get to grips with it, a bit like a learner driver trying too hard. So expect that it is going to take time to learn and some practices will be better than others. To help get the hang of it, schedule in a 10 minute practice session each day at a fixed time. Try also to apply it to actual panics. It is important to remember, though, that the breathing routine is a useful way of staying around long enough to realize that what you fear most is not going to happen. To remind you of what is important in the breathing retraining perhaps we could all write down on a slip of paper that you carry with you:

1. slowness of breathing;
2. abdominal breathing;
3. brief pause after each breathing phase.

There are other techniques for helping you hang in there and we will discuss them in later sessions.

It should be noted from the above that it is not simply a matter of teaching panic disorder clients breathing retraining, there are many cognitive elements, particularly the challenging of safety-seeking beliefs ('I am only safe if . . .'), that are needed for successful implementation of the strategy.

Abstaining from safety-seeking behaviours

Safety-seeking behaviours are a product of safety-seeking beliefs. Probably the most common belief amongst panic disorder clients with moderate to severe agoraphobic avoidance is 'I am only safe at home'. In this session clients are encouraged to test out these beliefs by, for example, staying where a panic occurs long enough to collect sufficient information to give the lie to the belief, e.g. 'Well I have not run for home yet and I am still in one piece, maybe it is not absolutely true that I am only safe at home, I'll stay a while longer to see what happens. For now, I will count the number of cans of beans on the supermarket shelf.' In this example counting cans of beans on the shelf is a coping response but the same technique would constitute an avoidance response if it had not first of all been placed in the context of attempting to disconfirm a belief. (It should be noted that this differs from the traditional behavioural injunction to simply stay until the fear has subsided.)

At the end of this session clients are asked, for homework, to practise Items (1) and (2) from the Monitoring Panic Attacks handout (Figure 5.2) and to monitor their panic attacks (Figure 5.3).

Session Two (Core). A: Review Monitoring Panic Attacks, Breathing Retraining and the Challenging of Safety Beliefs. B: Performance of Feared Activities

The session begins with a review of the previous session's homework. The group leader first asks clients individually about the frequency and intensity of any panic attacks. When Sara was asked about her panic attacks the following exchange took place.

Sara. You don't really want to know. I was OK leaving here last week, then two days later on a Sunday afternoon, when there is virtually no traffic about, I crash the car! I have not been out since until today, I have been having panics all the time at home.

Co-leader. How much damage was done?

Sara. I suddenly decided to turn right, didn't signal and the car behind dented my rear bumper. Fortunately he was going slow because he was looking for an address. I have some whiplash.

Leader. This shows how stresses can increase the frequency of panic attacks. One way forward is to ask yourself whether the hassle that has just happened is a mountain or a molehill or somewhere in between. If you continue to look at the hassle as a mountain you are more likely to have panic attacks.

Many of the strategies recommended for use in the group programme for generalized anxiety disorder (Chapter 4) such as 'mountain . . . molehill' continua are useful to introduce, at least in passing, to the panic disorder group in order to help modify background stressors that are often the precipitants for an increased frequency of panic attacks. In group work, just as in individual counselling, it is important to focus on what is uppermost in a client's mind and use the data of their experience to illustrate general points. However, in a group it is essential that the details of their difficulty are not elaborated upon to the point that it ceases to be a learning experience for other members. The group discussion continues.

Sara. But not driving to me is a 'mountain', it was the one place I felt safe, otherwise I am a prisoner.

Co-leader. But being safe is only about taking reasonable care. You don't normally walk across the road with your eyes down ignoring the traffic, do you?

Sara. I see what you mean, I was thinking more about getting back home for a TV programme than about my driving.

John. I go across the road like that with my eyes down.

Leader. Why is that John?

John. I don't know, sitting here it is crazy!

Leader. Just close your eyes, imagine beginning to cross the road outside and try and guess at what it sounds as if you are saying to yourself to make you keep your eyes on the ground.

John. It's weird: 'I am safe if I can't see what is coming'.

Stan. Jesus! my two year old does that, covers his eyes and thinks I can't catch him if he can't see me.

Leader. Many of the beliefs that make for safety-seeking behaviours are like that, they belong way back, and we are hardly aware and often embarrassed to find ourselves operating on them.

Sara. Mine just seem to come and I am not thinking anything.

Co-leader. Did you manage to write them down on the panic form?

Sara. No, I have just been out of the game.

Leader. Maybe we have to put a turnstile on your panics Sara, let one through at a time, do a standback assessment of it, and try and discover the thoughts that are fuelling it and test out the thoughts, before letting the next one through.

Sara. But I don't want to let any through! The day after the accident I tried to keep very calm, sat still, had relaxing music on and got my mother to look after the baby and it made no difference.

Leader. The problem is that sitting still and organizing your day in the way you did is a safety-seeking behaviour, it is as if you had said to yourself 'I am only safe if I do not go out, sit still all day, etc.' You have really conducted an experiment and shown that if you engage in safety-seeking behaviours, it does not work, you still have panics.

Sara. I would have been worse if I had not asked my mum to look after the baby and had gone out.

Leader. But you don't know that if you had tried to stay in the situation using the breathing retraining, that you would not have discovered that nothing terrible was going to happen.

Stan. I found the breathing retraining very useful for my night time panic attacks, they are still happening just as often but they do not bother me as much now.

Co-leader. What were your scores on them Stan?

Stan. I have had three since we last met and there were two sevens and an eight.

Co-leader. That's great, the Form (Figure 5.3) can show you the progress you're making.

John. It seems to be all about living dangerously.

Leader. Ah but is it really living dangerously, John?

John. (laughing) Well I tell you this, if I see any of you at my funeral . . .

The second part of this session is devoted to the performance of feared activities.

Leader. On the subject of living dangerously, could we look at Item (3) on the Handout (Figure 5.2). We are suggesting there that you deliberately try to make the thing that you fear most happen.

John. You have to be joking!

Co-leader. If you don't try to make the thing you fear most happen, then you never truly realize that it is an impossibility. Say you fear being in a supermarket queue because you think that you will faint, try to deliberately faint there.

John. You would look a fool if I did!

Co-leader. I would bet you £5 that you could not faint in a supermarket queue if you tried.

John. Hmm, this is dodgy, can I have my wife with me?

Co-leader. Not quite, she is always with you, and you are likely to operate on the safety belief that you were really safe because she was with you.

John. But I will not be able to get to the supermarket unless she is with me.

Co-leader. OK, she has to wait outside whilst you try and faint in a queue inside.

Leader. What I would like is for everybody to make at least one attempt to make their worst horror come true and we could plan it now in the way we have John's – don't all run for the door!

Another way of helping panic clients disconfirm their predictions is to have them identify four challenges they could tackle before the next session (it does not matter if a challenge is duplicated across participants). Specify the challenges in advance, indicating: the degree of fear, on a scale 0–10 (high score most fearful), that they anticipate having during the task; the likelihood of a panic attack; and the anticipated degree of safety, on a scale 0–10 (high score very unsafe). After the task they record the actual fear experienced, whether they had a panic attack, and their belief in their safety in the particular situation. The details can be recorded on the Expectations vs Experience form of Figure 5.5.

EXPECTATIONS vs EXPERIENCES

Situation 1 ....
....

Expected fear (0–10) ...... Likelihood of a panic attack (0–10) ......
Expected safety (0–10) ...... Do you expect to have a panic attack? Yes .... No ....

Experienced fear (0–10) ....   Did you have a panic attack? Yes ..... No .....
Safety estimate (0–10) ....

Situation 2 ....
....

Expected fear (0–10) ...... Likelihood of a panic attack (0–10) ......
Expected safety (0–10) ...... Do you expect to have a panic attack? Yes .... No ....

Experienced fear (0–10) ...... Did you have a panic attack? Yes .... No ....
Safety estimate (0–10) ......

Situation 3 ....
....

Expected fear (0–10) ...... Likelihood of a panic attack (0–10) ......
Expected safety (0–10) ...... Do you expect to have a panic attack? Yes .... No ....

Experienced fear (0–10) ...... Did you have a panic attack? Yes .... No ....
Safety estimate (0–10) ......

Situation 4 ....
....

Expected fear (0–10) ...... Likelihood of a panic attack (0–10) ......
Expected safety (0–10) ...... Do you expect to have a panic attack? Yes .... No ....

Experienced fear (0–10) ...... Did you have a panic attack? Yes .... No ....
Safety estimate (0–10) ....

[*Note:* A higher score means more fear, more unsafe and the greater likelihood of a panic attack.]

Figure 5.5   Expectations vs Experiences Form

Completion of the Expectations vs Experiences Form reminds clients of
the mismatch between expectations and experiences and overall they
become less fearful in situations that historically have evoked panic.
However, if a client predicts no panic in a situation and does experience a panic attack they are likely to be more fearful on the next
challenge. It should be stressed that the goal is to make them better
predictors and to reduce the gap between expectations and experience,
so that they are not so wound up by the time they come to a situation
that this produces unusual bodily sensations which are then catastrophically misinterpreted. But they have to accept that on occasion,
to begin with at least, a positive prediction may be wrong.

The second part of this session is devoted to ensuring that between
sessions clients practise for at least 3 hours a week performing activities that they have previously avoided. The rationale given is that
one needs to devote at least this much time each week to the task in
order to feel that one is moving forward. An analogy may be drawn
with physical exercise: in order to feel that one was becoming
physically fit one would probably need to devote about three hours a
week. To help ensure compliance with this homework, clients are introduced to the Overcoming Feared Situations form shown in Figure
5.6 and asked to complete it between sessions.

In the session, clients are asked to construct a ladder. The bottom rung
is a task that they can just complete with moderate difficulty and the
top rung represents the goal that they wish to achieve by the end of the
programme. Sara constructed the ladder of Figure 5.7.

Clients are then asked to label the intermediate rungs by asking themselves what would be half-way, in terms of difficulty, between the top
and bottom rungs, then specifying steps between the middle and bottom and the middle and top. It is explained that this is only a very
rough training programme, and that it is almost impossible to know in
advance what size steps should be taken so that the inability to climb a
particular rung between sessions should not be seen as failure but
simply as indicating that an intermediate step has to be introduced. In
this way clients are inoculated against 'failure experiences'. The 3
hours practice between sessions should include material appropriate
to the particular rung, together with other material that would give a
sense of achievement. In Sara's case she agreed that in addition to
walking to her local shops each day when it was quiet, on Sunday

OVERCOMING FEARED SITUATIONS

We find that in order to begin to get their confidence back people need to spend about three hours a week tackling some of the situations that they have been avoiding. What counts is the time you spend alone in the feared situation. For example, you might have been avoiding shopping in town and decide to take a trip to town with a friend. The time to be counted would be the time you spent alone in a shop, away from your friend. Keep a diary of your training. Try to practice daily.

Week 1

	What I did	Time alone	Max. anxiety (0–10)
1			
2			
3			
4			
5			
6			
7			

Week's Total Practice   Time ....

Week 2

	What I did	Time alone	Max. anxiety (0–10)
1			
2			
3			
4			
5			
6			
7			

Week's Total Practice   Time ....

Week 3

	What I did	Time alone	Max. anxiety (0–10)
1			
2			
3			
4			
5			
6			
7			

Week's Total Practice   Time ....

Figure 5.6   Overcoming Feared Situations

Figure 5.7 Sara's Ladder

morning she would drive with her husband to an almost deserted industrial estate and spend an hour driving around.

The construction of the ladders is more difficult when there is little or no agoraphobic avoidance, but it is unusual for there not to be at least some agoraphobic avoidance. Where agoraphobic avoidance is minimal, special attention can be focused on managing the panics without recourse to a safety-seeking behaviour during them. For example, Jane claimed that she did not attempt to escape from any situation when her panic attacks occurred. But further examination revealed that when the attacks occurred at home she would go and lie down on her stomach with a cushion underneath in order, she believed, to prevent herself being sick. Consequently the first rung of her ladder was to let herself experience panics at home without using this strategy. The top rung of her ladder was to return to work and not apologize to colleagues for her panic symptoms.

Sessions Three to Five. Revision of Materials in First Two Sessions, Alternative Ways of Checking Out the Panic Forecast

The third session begins with a review of the previous session's homework. In the following extract a client's depression is sabotaging his training programme and ways of circumventing this are discussed.

Stan. I managed the first rung on my ladder, driving to the local chemist and DIY shop but for the last few days I have not done anything.
Leader. Why is that?

Stan. I started thinking of what I used to be able to do. I was never like this. Used to be life and soul of the party. Now I haven't got a job, can't afford to look for Christmas presents for the nephews and nieces.

Leader. Would they enjoy it if you were able to play a ball game with them in the park or take them for a swim?

Stan. Oh yes.

Leader. Well could not that be one of the rungs on the ladder?

Stan. I just think back.

Co-leader. When athletes are running a marathon they keep their eyes focused on a spot about 100 metres ahead, and tell themselves that they just have to reach that spot. When they get there they tell themselves well done and select another spot 100 metres ahead. That is the only way they can finish the race. If they think back to what they once did or how far there is to go to the end of the race they are less likely to finish. In the same way the next rung of the ladder is your 100-metre mark.

Here again the strategies used to motivate clients to perform feared activities are replete with metaphor – climbing a ladder and running a race – so that in effect they are writing a story of their endeavours. The evolving story then guides their actions.

Breathing retraining as described in the previous session is a means to an end and not an end in itself and sometimes it can prove a distraction, as in Jane's case.

Jane. I stopped myself lying down when I felt panicky at home, but I got so frustrated trying to tune my breathing in that I was sick. Getting the rhythm of anything I find very difficult and I could not manage the ten minute breathing retraining practices.

Co-leader. There are two alternative strategies that people can use to help stay in the situation they fear:

(a) Press on one eye as you breathe out. It can look like you have something in your eye if you are in public. This slows your breathing down.

(b) Take a deep breath and tense your stomach muscles and increase the pressure in your chest. This leads to a slight increase in heart rate followed by a drop of about 20 beats per minute within 2–3 seconds.

Perhaps we could try these now, so that you have a menu of options to choose from.

The focus then shifted to the veracity of forecasts made by clients during their panics.

Leader. What I want to look at now are the thoughts people have during their panic attacks. One or more of the following themes (see Greenberg, 1989) is usually present:

1.   vulnerability – 'I am vulnerable to harm';
2.   escalation – 'Symptoms will escalate into something worse';
3.   copelessness – 'I can't control symptoms or cope with the problem on my own.'

Could I start with your Panic Monitoring Form (Figure 5.3), Stan? I notice that you thought that you were going to have a heart attack.
Stan. I always think that during a panic.
Leader. Do you believe it sitting here now?
Stan. Not as much, because I am not breathless.
Leader. So when you are breathless you make a wrong forecast?
Stan. Well I suppose I do, but my father died of a heart attack.
Leader. How old was he?
Stan. Seventy-six.
Leader. And you are how old, Stan?
Stan. I take your point but you never know.
Co-leader. I don't think you can know with absolute certainty but there has to be a difference between what is possible and what is probable. You avoid or are very cautious when something is probable but not when it is just possible.
Stan. I think all my worrying about having a heart attack is going to bring one on.
Leader. That is a good example of both escalation and vulnerability.
Co-leader. What about deliberately trying to bring on the thing you most fear, the heart attack, Stan? You could start here by running up and down the stairs, do a few press ups. If you are truly vulnerable this should escalate into a heart attack.
Stan. Aren't I sorry I came today!
John. (laughing) It's good for you Stan, I would like to see this.
Leader. Actually, John, you have put on the form that in the shop you felt that everything was closing in on you and you escaped. That

sounds like an example of copelessness. Maybe you would like to test this out by spending two minutes in the broom cupboard whilst John does his vigorous exercise and has a heart attack.

John. Game, set and match!

The in-session testing out of worst fears can serve as a stepping stone for an out-of-session disconfirmation exercise. But the in-session exercises rarely serve as a substitute for the homework disconfirmation exercises since clients often feel that they must be safe because they are in the presence of the counsellors. It is of course possible to challenge this 'magical' influence of the counsellor by asking clients to explain, for example, how the group leaders prevented them having a heart attack, given that their heart was so weak and their exercise so vigorous.

Sessions Six to Eight. Review of Progress, Tackling Avoided Situations, Challenging of Panic Beliefs and Interoceptive Exercises

Review of progress, tackling avoided situations

The progress of clients in tackling avoided situations is best monitored by splitting the group into two with the leader taking one half of the group and the co-leader the other half. It is important for the leaders to have identical copies of the homework assignments that were set previously. The homeworks would have specified (a) an attempted deliberate induction of a panic, (b) four disconfirmation experiments and (c) details of the 3 hours or more training per week.

An open question, such as 'How are things?', addressed to the subgroup usually elicits the report of a success experience from some member. It is important to focus on the positive first, to praise the achievement, and encourage the client to make explicit how they navigated past potential trouble spots. In this way clients can serve as coping models for other group members so that group counselling is not simply individual counselling in a group, as the following exchange shows.

Sara. I am quite pleased with myself. I have been going to the local shops when they are busy without any great difficulty.

Co-leader. Great, how long is it since you have been able to do that?

Sara. Must be over a year now.

Co-leader. That's a grand achievement after such a time.

Sara. Yes!

Co-leader. But you mentioned that you had some difficulty.

Sara. It was just that on the Saturday afternoon I saw some teenagers stealing by the checkout. My heart sank. I thought 'Why does it always go wrong for me, car crash, now robberies?' But I signalled to the girl on the checkout and she got the store detective. I was pleased with myself in the end.

Co-leader. So that instead of just saying 'It's awful, it's not fair that I should be involved in further hassles,' you took action.

Jane. That is where I have bottled out. I have managed to get back to work, which was the next rung on my ladder, but I lost my nerve when asked to make a presentation on the use of some new software and made ridiculous excuses not to. I suppose I felt it's not fair asking me when I have just come back, but then that's stupid because my colleagues are so nice. I think it is because I went off work originally with a panic that occurred on the morning prior to a presentation.

Co-leader. It sounds as if you are saying to yourself that because you have had a bad panic in that situation before you will have one again. That's just the sort of thing we need to monitor on the Expectations vs Experiences form (Figure 5.5). How would you cope with beginning to panic in the presentation?

Jane. Well I suppose that at worst I could go to the toilet for a few minutes and tune my breathing in.

Co-leader. Certainly that could be a start, to eventually not having any 'arm bands' and staying in the situation and seeing that nothing awful happens. Perhaps this could be one of your challenges before the next session.

Jane. OK.

Co-leader. I'll just write that down.

The 'failures' of clients can easily depress a group, so before they are addressed the successes should be elaborated. The first step for the leaders in addressing failures is to nip in the bud the 'awfulizing' that makes for problem disorientation, then to refine the problem so that the core panic belief is exposed, and finally to problem-solve a range of solutions. The range will include the optimal solution of simply asking the client to stay in the situation and find that nothing catastrophic happens, and less optimal solutions – such as breathing retraining – which contain ways of helping the individual remain 'afloat' in the situation but risk a dependence that might backfire in the long term. As the sessions progress, clients are asked to increasingly use the more optimal solutions.

Challenging panic beliefs

Prior to these sessions the leader and co-leader review the Panic Monitoring Forms (Figure 5.3) to determine the most commonly occurring panic beliefs that group members experience during panic attacks. There is often a gap between how much the panic belief is believed away from the situation and how much it is believed during a panic. The therapeutic task is to make available to the client in a panic the type of thinking that occurs in their 'better moments.'

The group leaders distilled the panic beliefs of Figure 5.8 from the Forms. These are then discussed in the group. Members are asked which beliefs they totally believe during a panic, then how much they believe them sitting in the group. Usually clients are less certain of the panic belief away from the experience and they are then asked to elaborate on why they are less certain. The reasons for the less than 100 per cent certainty in a panic belief are summarized and put on a prompt card to be used in the event of a panic. There are three ways in which a panic belief can be challenged.

A three-dimensional challenge of panic beliefs
1. *Authority.* Client's panic beliefs seem to them self-evidently true, the counsellor may not be perceived as a particularly credible

---

GROUP PANIC BELIEFS

1. If people see me having a panic they will lose respect.

2. A panic can drive me insane.

3. It could be dangerous to carry on my usual activities during a panic.

4. I can't deal with panicky feelings on my own.

5. If I can't control my anxiety perfectly I'm a failure.

6. I have to keep hurrying to avoid a panic attack.

Figure 5.8   Group Panic Beliefs

source on their veracity, not having experienced panic attacks. Individual counselling for panic disorder can result in a polarization – the client endorsing the panic belief, the counsellor contradicting it. In the group the client is more likely to be exposed to shades of opinion on the panic belief and, removed from a 'You win, I lose' battle, the client can gradually assimilate the cognitive changes.

2. *Validity*.The validity of a panic belief may be tested by conducting a behavioural experiment either during the sessions or as a homework exercise. It is important, however, that the experiment is conducted without long-term recourse to any safety-seeking behaviour that the client uses privately to invalidate the disconfirmation.

3. *Utility*. Panic beliefs can also be questioned in terms of whether they frustrate the attainment of goals.

Skill in the use of the three-dimensional challenge of panic beliefs lies in shifting from one dimension to another rather than pursuing one dimension relentlessly.

Jane. That's what I do, rush all the time, so I don't have a panic.
Co-leader. Does it work? (Utility)
Jane. Well no, but I would have even more, if I didn't rush.
Co-leader. How do you know? Have you ever tried not rushing? (Validity)
Jane. It's just my personality.
Sara. I would be exhausted if I went at your pace. (Credible authority)
Jane. Now and again I just have to go and lie down and I have got things to do.
Sara. There's always tomorrow, maybe you would have more energy for something pleasant. (Utility) I just worry about making a fool of myself when I panic outside.
Leader. Others probably think at most that you are physically unwell, that you ate a dodgy pork pie! (Validity)
John. When I went back to the barbers, I apologized for getting in such a state last time and he just looked at me with an open mouth, he hadn't realized that. (Validity)
Co-leader. Have you ever made a fool of yourself, Sara?
Sara. No, I don't think so, but I might.
Co-leader. So even yourself you don't think you have made a fool of yourself. (Authority)
Sara. No, but I stop myself by hanging on to something or someone for grim death.

Leader. That's what we want to encourage you to stop doing, to see if anything awful happens. (Validity)

Sara. I get my younger sister to stay off school and be with me on my worst days. She is collecting me after the group. She is very bright, more sensible than me. I want her to do well but . . .

Stan. Keeping her off school isn't going to help her or you. (Utility) My wife will pick you up, I am sure, and take you back, we don't live that far from you, it's no problem for us, honestly.

In the above extract there are not only challenges to the authority, validity and utility by which panic beliefs are held but there are also examples of modelling alternative cognitive processes by group members and an extension of group support to the natural setting.

Interoceptive exercises in group session and at home

Building up a client's tolerance of unusual bodily sensations represents the other side of the coin to training them not to catastrophically misinterpret bodily sensations. The evidence to date seems to suggest that both are effective in the treatment of panic disorder and the most parsimonious solution seems to be to incorporate both into a panic programme. Some clients may find one approach more useful than the other.

In the session the leader takes the group through a series of exercises to determine which most closely evoke the panic sensations, these are then practised as a homework exercise. Some useful interoceptive exercises are given in Figure 5.9.

INTEROCEPTIVE EXERCISES

1. Shake head from side to side for 30 seconds.
2. Breathe deeply and quickly 20–30 breaths a minute for one minute, i.e., hyperventilate.
3. Place head between legs for 30 seconds and lift head.
4. Hold breath for 30 seconds.
5. Run on spot for one minute.
6. Stare at a dot for a minute then read.

Figure 5.9 Interoceptive Exercises

The effects of each exercise should be discussed in the group before moving on to the next exercise. This provides an important way of accessing any catastrophic cognitions that may only be available to consciousness at the actual time of panic. If a client does become particularly distressed then the salient cognitions are more likely to come to the fore and can be dealt with. In some instances a client might refuse to perform a particular exercise. This can be tackled by asking them to perform the exercise for less time than other group members and seeing if there is any effect. This gives them a sense of control over the exercise whilst at the same time making the point experientially that the panic-like sensations can have a very simple non-threatening explanation. Further, the inadvertent use of some such exercise can be invoked as an explanatory mechanism for some client's 'out of the blue' panic attacks, often the most frightening.

Jane. My panics are so stupid, the other night I am enjoying watching a soap on TV, then when it had finished, I started.
Co-leader. Was it a good episode?
Jane. Yes it was great, that's why I can't see why it should have happened.
Co-leader. I have noticed that you do sigh a lot, and maybe if it was that good you were holding your breath, this causes you to gulp in air at the end of the programme, and then you only have your bodily sensations to watch. You become even more alarmed at your panic symptoms because there is no apparent reason for them.
Jane. What, the sighing and holding my breath produces the feelings?
Co-leader. Yes.
Stan. Well, what about my having an attack in my sleep?
Co-leader. Perhaps you were dreaming of something that briefly made you hold your breath, then you gulped air in.
Stan. (laughing) See, women at the root of it all again!
Leader. Even just lying there with your chest constricted could cause you to start gulping in air and lead on to a panic.

For some people the panic triggers are quite idiosyncratic, for example fluorescent lights or a hot stuffy room, and where possible those conditions should be replicated in the group situation as a prelude to homework. In instances where clients are experiencing derealisation – the sensation when outside that they are walking on pillows and that the buildings on either side of the road are closing in on them – they can be encouraged to walk briefly outside without any safety-seeking behaviour, such as holding onto or being close to railings, and test out whether the buildings do actually graze them. It is then suggested that they remind themselves that the derealization is as much an illusion as a stick dipped into water appearing bent.

For homework, clients are asked to spend 10 minutes a day on their interoceptive exercises, pausing briefly between each exercise. (It should be noted that the use of interoceptive exercises here has a different rationale to the same exercises used in interoceptive exposure as originally developed by Barlow and Cerny (1988), who suggested using each exercise for 10–30 seconds longer than the point at which the person becomes uncomfortable. Each exercise is repeated until there is a significant decrement in anxiety – i.e. the authors were working within an exposure paradigm. Though their theoretical rationale may be different, the difference in what clients actually do for homework may be more apparent than real.)

Sessions Nine, Ten and Follow-ups. Concluding Sessions

These sessions should include, first, a revision of all that has been taught on the course and a highlighting by group members of those aspects that are most salient for them. A coping model of future operation should be emphasized rather than an expectation that they should be masters of every situation. Completing the programme can be likened to the client just having passed their driving test. They are likely to be still fearful 'on the road', perhaps even more so initially because they will not have the support of others. However, further improvements are likely as they practise their skills. In the first couple of months, particularly, there are likely to be some scary moments, but these must be regarded as learning opportunities. Assessment of the clients on the various self-report symptom measures should be undertaken at the final session and, again, at the follow-up sessions to assist in auditing the effectiveness of the programme.

Clients should be encouraged to map out what would be their week-by-week targets over the next six weeks. It is recommended that there be booster sessions at six weeks and three months, both as a way of lessening dependence and of providing reassurance. The booster sessions do not need to be homogenous, though it is easier for the counsellors if they are. In routine practice it is usually difficult to maintain a sufficient number of group members of any one disorder for a viable group during follow-up. A more heterogeneous group makes for less dependence and becomes viable because members have already learnt a common cognitive model.

6

ANXIETY DISORDERS 3: POSTTRAUMATIC STRESS DISORDER

Extreme traumas have long been thought of as precipitants for a distinct pattern of symptom responses. In Homer's *Odyssey*, warriors' diaries revealed gruelling accounts of intense panic and disturbance both during and following battlefield encounters (Trimble 1985). The two world wars introduced a variety of synonyms for traumatic stress such as shell shock, war neurosis, combat exhaustion and fight fatigue. However, it was not until 1980 that these terms were subsumed under the heading of posttraumatic stress disorder (PTSD) and diagnostic criteria elaborated (American Psychiatric Association 1980). Studies on non-combat populations such as survivors of fire, explosion, flood and concentration camps showed them also to be experiencing PTSD symptoms (Scott and Stradling 1992). But probably most clients suffering debility from extreme trauma have not been involved in a battle, noteworthy disaster or an incident that grabbed newspaper headlines, rather they are more commonly victims of a motor vehicle accident or an assault. Recent data from the US National Comorbidity Study (Kessler *et al*. 1996) indicates PTSD lifetime prevalence rates at about 5 per cent and 10 per cent among American men and women respectively.

The most recent revision of PTSD criteria is contained in the Diagnostic and Statistical Manual of Mental Disorders, 4th edition (DSM IV – American Psychiatric Association 1994: see Appendix A) which gives the stressor criterion, Criterion A, for PTSD of Figure 6.1.

Criterion A acts as the gateway to PTSD in that even if a person has all the symptoms of PTSD they cannot be diagnosed as suffering from the condition unless they meet the stressor criterion. The first part of

Criterion A. Stressor.
The person has been exposed to a traumatic event in which both of the
following were present:

1. The person experienced, witnessed, or was confronted with an event
   or events that involved actual or threatened death or serious injury, or
   a threat to the physical integrity of self or others.
2. The person's response involved intense fear, helplessness, or horror.

Figure 6.1   Stressor Criterion for PTSD

Criterion A acknowledges that the stressor must be objectively extreme
whilst the second part signifies that it must also have been subjectively
experienced as extreme.

DSM IV groups the symptoms of PTSD under the five further headings
given in Figure 6.2.

The distinction between PTSD and acute stress disorder is made because there is a great deal of naturally occurring improvement in

Criterion B. Intrusion
The traumatic event is persistently re-experienced in one or more of
five* possible ways.

Criterion C. Avoidance
Persistent avoidance of stimuli associated with the trauma and numbing
of general responsiveness, as indicated by three or more of seven*
possible ways.

Criterion D. Disordered arousal
Persistent symptoms of increased arousal as indicated by two or more
of five* possible ways.

Criterion E. Duration
Symptoms listed under criteria B, C and D must have lasted more than 1
month.
(If criteria A–D are met but symptoms have lasted less than a month
then the term acute stress disorder is used instead.)

Criterion F. Functional impairment
The disturbance causes clinically significant distress or impairment in
social, occupational, or other important areas of functioning.

(*see Appendix A)

Figure 6.2   Criteria B to F for PTSD

trauma victims' symptoms in the weeks and months immediately following the trauma. For example, Rothbaum *et al.* (1992) found that while 94 per cent of women entering a longitudinal study following rape met criteria for PTSD at approximately 2 weeks post-rape, this had reduced to about 50 per cent at 12 weeks. Similarly, Blanchard *et al.* (1995) reported that one half of patients suffering from PTSD after a motor vehicle accident were recovered by 6 months. There is, then, a great deal of natural adaptation to extreme trauma. The US National Co-Morbidity Study (Kessler *et al.* 1996) showed that whilst 75 per cent of the population are likely to experience a Criterion A stressor, the lifetime prevalence of PTSD is only 7.5 per cent. If the mechanism by which these adjustments are made can be understood then this may have important implications for those suffering long-term debility – chronic PTSD. What is it, then, that successful adapters are able to do that others are not?

It is suggested that the primary mechanism involved in successful interaction with the trauma memory is a shift from a primarily perceptual or primitive mode of processing to a more conceptual mode, relocating the trauma experience into the context of an overall benign life experience. This adaptive interaction takes place at two levels:

(a)   the trauma itself – in which the client shifts from a primarily perceptual processing, e.g. 'His eyes were just bulging out of his head as he hung there, staring right through me', to a primarily conceptual level, e.g. 'At least I did all I could to help him';
(b)   the typicality of the trauma, in which the trauma is seen as an exception to previous life experiences and of little or no relevance to the future.

Initial difficulties in contextualizing the trauma arise because in the immediate aftermath the visuo-spatial and verbal stores in working memory dictate actions, reversing the normal hierarchy between the stores and the central executive. The restoration of the central executive requires a switch to a more conceptual mode of processing. It is well established that those with a previous history of emotional disorder are more likely to suffer PTSD in the wake of an extreme trauma. This finding is consistent with the above model in that those with a psychiatric history are more likely to interpret their trauma as typical of their benighted life pattern and a further justification for their subsequent hypervigilance.

Perhaps the key difference between survivors of trauma who do and do not develop PTSD is that the former are hypervigilant. (The hyper-vigilance is associated with an exaggerated startle response. Together with increased irritability these represent hallmarks of PTSD under Criterion D – symptoms of disordered arousal). The vigilance–hypervigilance dimension is likely to be salient from an evolutionary perspective. The maintenance of a hypervigilant state requires justi-fication, and this is furnished by the graphic intrusive imagery of the trauma. These images are toxic and consequently there is a tendency to avoid them, but this avoidance means that they are not properly con-textualized. Hypervigilance brings preoccupation, preventing the per-formance of previously valued roles and the pursuit of previous life goals, typically leading to irritability and a concomitant deterioration of relationships.

The most common model of stress is a transactional one (see Meichen-baum 1985, and Figure 4.1), in which stress is regarded neither as a property of the individual nor of the environment but of the interaction between them. Accordingly, whether a particular person has a PTSD response to a trauma will depend not only on the extremity of the trauma (e.g., did they lose a close relative? were they seriously physically injured with likely long-term debility?) but also on various aspects of the individual (e.g. have they had previous extreme trauma? were there previous emotional problems?). Thus an individual may respond unfavourably to a less extreme trauma if they have a number of personal vulnerability factors. By contrast, some events, e.g. rape, are so extremely intrusive that they would evoke an initial traumatic response in almost anybody. Here, however, the individual factors may exert an important influence on recovery.

In traditional cognitive–behavioural approaches to the treatment of PTSD the individual has been regarded as in need of exposure to the full memory of the trauma for as long as it takes to produce a habitua-tion response. Therapeutic efforts have been devoted almost entirely to ensuring adequate exposure with little regard for the uniqueness of the individual and their history. Theoretical formulations such as those of Foa and Kozak (1986) acknowledge that the end result of interventions has to be that the individual comes to ascribe a more adaptive meaning to the trauma and their response to it, but have been unclear as to why prolonged exposure was the *sine qua non* for providing the necessary corrective information.

From a biological perspective it appears that in extreme trauma high levels of cortisol may be released which can damage the hippocampus. One of the functions of the hippocampus appears to be to coordinate the various sensory aspects of an experience, the smells, sights, etc., locate the experience in space and time, and provide an overall meaning. PTSD clients appear to have a smaller hippocampal volume than non-PTSD survivors of trauma (Van der Kolk 1996). Thus PTSD clients are likely to have a more fragmented memory of the trauma. The amygdala registers affect-laden memories, and these are usually kept in check by the hippocampus, but damage to the hippocampus from cortisol release would prevent this. Cortisol damage to the hippocampus is thought to be reversible.

INITIAL ASSESSMENT

For patients recently traumatized – within the previous few weeks – a group debriefing is probably the appropriate response whether they meet the actual criteria for acute stress disorder or not. The rationale for a debriefing is that early intervention may prevent the development of more serious problems later, particularly PTSD. But there is little evidence of its effectiveness overall (Kenardy et al. 1996) and whether it exerts a preventive function may depend on the type of debriefing. Guidelines for conducting a de-briefing are given in Scott and Stradling (1992) and are based on the premise that no pressure should be exerted on anyone to disclose their thoughts or feelings. After the debriefing people are given a contact number should their symptoms not resolve. Though there is a strong humanitarian case for making professional services available to victims in the wake of a trauma, the goal should be to enhance individuals' natural coping mechanisms.

Given the improvements in PTSD symptoms that often occur in the first 6 months post trauma, it is probably a better use of resources to restrict a group programme to those who were traumatized at least 6 months earlier, though exceptionally one might admit clients traumatized as recently as 3 months ago.

The assessment interview should be structured around the DSM IV criteria for PTSD (see Appendix A) with appropriate questions asked under each heading. There are well-validated structured interviews for PTSD such as the Clinician Administered PTSD Scale (CAPS: Blake *et al.* 1990) but they are time consuming, the CAPS typically taking an hour for clients who prove to have PTSD and 30–40 minutes for those who do not. It is useful to have a category of sub-syndromal PTSD. The commonest presentation of sub-syndromal PTSD is of insufficient avoidance symptoms for a diagnosis of PTSD but sufficient of the other two symptom clusters – intrusion and disordered arousal. Sub-syndromal clients can benefit from a couple of individual counselling sessions focusing on their prominent symptom clusters but a group programme is usually too extensive an intervention for them. Material can be extracted from the group programme given below that addresses the particular concerns of the individual sub-syndromal client. It is important that these clients are not dismissed simply because they do not meet full PTSD criteria and that their needs are addressed in a systematic way, because even sub-syndromal PTSD can greatly restrict an individual's activities and relationships.

Posttraumatic stress disorder is a disorder with considerable co-morbidity, the (US) National Comorbidity Survey (Kessler *et al.* 1996) suggesting a lifetime prevalence of major depression of 48 per cent, alcohol or drug abuse 65 per cent, generalized anxiety disorder 16 per cent and panic disorder 11 per cent. Screening for other disorders is therefore important. If there is an addiction, treatment of this is necessary before addressing the PTSD. Often the client is using the alcohol or drugs to block out the memories and ensure sleep, so that though they may be willing to attend a PTSD group they may be unwilling to abstain first. It is recommended that in such cases the client's needs are addressed in individual counselling.

Groups can be homogeneous with regard to the original trauma, e.g. consisting entirely of rape victims. In routine practice most counsellors will have a mixed PTSD caseload of motor vehicle accident victims, those who have been variously assaulted, and survivors of disasters. The programme described here is for such a mixed group, but that is not to say it is not perfectly valid to run a group exclusively for, say, incest survivors or combat veterans. A group mixed by trauma and sex is problematic for clients who have been the victim of a sexual assault and in the authors' view should be avoided.

AUDITING THE PTSD GROUP PROGRAMME

The PENN Inventory (PENN: Hammarberg 1992) covers all the PTSD symptoms and is a useful measure of change. The most commonly used PTSD outcome measure is the Impact of Event Scale (IES: Horowitz *et al.* 1979). However, it does not assess disordered arousal symptoms and should be more properly viewed as a stress response measure. Both instruments are reproduced in the appendices to Scott and Stradling (1992). The Modified PTSD Scale (Falsetti *et al.* 1993) is a PTSD self-report measure which asks questions about the frequency and severity of each of the 17 DSM PTSD symptoms. We have examined the diagnostic accuracy of these three measures (Scott *et al.* 1997) in a study in which 150 clients completed the instruments and were also assessed using the CAPS interview in conjunction with the DSM IV criteria. The PENN Inventory was the most accurate. Using a cut-off of 37, it gave false positives of 15 per cent and false negatives of 20 per cent. The Impact of Event Scale was the least reliable.

Because of the high incidence of moderate to severe depression amongst PTSD clients it is useful to also measure progress with a depression self-report measure such as the Beck Depression Inventory (Beck *et al.* 1961). Clients scoring highly on the BDI (26+) may have considerable trauma-related guilt and/or difficulty adjusting to the loss of some previously valued role in the wake of the trauma. The high levels of co-morbidity mean that the counsellor will often have to incorporate, within the PTSD group programme, strategies for other disorders that are described elsewhere in this book.

CONVEYING THE METAPHOR

Clients suffering from post-traumatic stress disorder often report that they are 'not the same person' as they were before, and in contrast to most other emotional disorders they suffer an abrupt discontinuity of identity. Close relatives and friends become acutely aware of this change. The autobiography of the PTSD client is typically in two halves. The first half relates to how they viewed themselves and their personal world up to the time of the trauma and the second half presents a very different, post-trauma, view of themselves and their world. Prior to the trauma clients usually assumed most situations were safe until proven otherwise. In the aftermath of trauma clients routinely assume danger and therefore engage in hypervigilance and avoidance behaviour. The treatment of PTSD involves assisting the client in rewriting their autobiography so that there is a consistent view of themselves and their personal world. This must come from contextualizing the trauma in their pre-trauma experiences.

Historically in the treatment of PTSD the tendency has been for counsellors to try and normalize a client's feelings by telling them that they are a normal emotional response to an abnormal situation, but this is only a partial and potentially misleading truth. Whilst virtually all persons exposed to an extreme trauma show PTSD reactions in the week or so afterwards, over half are no longer suffering PTSD 3–6 months later. This means that the 'normal' response is not to be in a state which merits consideration for admission to a PTSD counselling programme. The major goal of the programme is then to help them do what the other, 'recovered', victims of the trauma have done. In essence the client is told that they are engaged in a battle: either they learn to control (contextualize) the memory of the trauma or the memory will control them. The warring factions are their present self looking at life through the glasses of the experience of the trauma, and their pre-trauma, 'no glasses', self. The question is who will win, or at least what peace agreement may be brokered.

Because the PTSD client is viewed by themselves and by significant others as 'not the same person', they usually feel very isolated and communication is fraught. They are, however, often more at ease with other similarly traumatized victims and can identify with them, often saying of others' experiences 'I have been there'. For this reason a PTSD group programme can seem an attractive option to a client and can act as a stepping stone for reconnecting them to the world around them. Meeting other PTSD clients helps many to be able to put into words for the first time their emotional experience of PTSD.

Reconnecting the client with the world is a major goal of the programme and an important first step towards this is involving a partner, close friend or relative of the client in the initial interview. This significant other has to be warned not to take the changes in the client's behaviour – e.g. increased irritability – personally, how to act as a 'coach' using the handout material given to the client, and what the likely prognosis is. Armed with this information they can then mediate between the client and the client's personal world. Significant others may play an important role in helping those with PTSD reactions contextualize their trauma and this may be the most salient aspect of support post-trauma.

Engagement of the client and the significant other in the therapeutic process is facilitated by the counsellor providing a readily understandable post-trauma metaphor.

Leader. When you experience an extreme trauma it is as if the alarm in your nervous system is knocked. It is now in this position (use a pencil to illustrate, at 60° clockwise from the vertical) when it should be in that position (rotate the pencil to 60° anticlockwise from the vertical) and your alarm begins to go off for the slightest reason. With the alarm in this new position you are likely to get angry over the smallest thing, e.g. your partner not handing you a cup of coffee but placing it down on the table. One of the things we will teach you is how to begin to ignore the false alarms, so that you get on better with the people around you. But we cannot reset the alarm in one sweep (illustrate by a movement of pencil from +60° to -60°) it is always two steps forward and one back (again illustrate by movement of the pen through 20° and back 10°). It is rather like driving lessons: some weeks you think you are doing fine and are going to pass your test and then other weeks you think that you are not going to make it, but gradually you do make it.

Particular Problems in Engaging the PTSD Client

One of the difficulties with engaging PTSD clients in counselling is that sometimes they know of other trauma victims who have recovered without recourse to professional help and believe that they also ought to be able to do so by themselves. This can be tackled by explaining that some people are more vulnerable than others to the effects of trauma. The chief vulnerability factors for PTSD are listed in Figure 6.3.

Thus two individuals exposed to the same trauma but differing on any one or more of the above factors will likely have a different outcome. Some individuals may have so little vulnerability that it would take a very extreme trauma – say the loss of a close relative – to usher in PTSD, whilst a highly vulnerable individual experiencing, say, a minor

```
┌─────────────────────────────────────────────────────────┐
│                                                           │
│                  PTSD VULNERABILITY FACTORS               │
│                                                           │
│       1. Genetic                                          │
│                                                           │
│       2. Early deprivation                                │
│                                                           │
│       3. Prior psychiatric illness                        │
│                                                           │
│       4. Prior stress                                     │
│                                                           │
│       5. Personality factors                              │
│                                                           │
└─────────────────────────────────────────────────────────┘
```

Figure 6.3   PTSD Vulnerability Factors

car crash may suffer PTSD because of the way in which it reignites some past life-threatening trauma (prior stress) from which they thought they had recovered. Listing the vulnerability factors shows the client that their response to trauma cannot be divorced from their history.

Given that one of the symptom clusters in PTSD is disordered arousal, it may be that one of the salient personality factors that makes for vulnerability is a predisposition to emotional arousability. Coren's (1988) Arousability Predisposition Scale has 12 items which include 'Sudden changes of any kind produce an immediate emotional effect on me', 'I find that my heart keeps beating fast for a while after I have been stirred up', 'I startle easily', and 'I am easily frustrated.' Emotional arousability may also be an important determinant not only of onset of PTSD but also of recovery.

Some clients' excessive self-blame can militate against engagement and they frequently say 'It is not as if I had any physical injury'. This point can be dealt with by telling clients that it seems that PTSD victims have a slightly reduced (4–12 per cent) hippocampal volume compared to non-PTSD survivors of trauma and this probably relates to their difficulty in handling the memory. But the damage caused to the hippocampus in extreme trauma is not necessarily irreversible. So they are not responsible for the problem of suffering their condition any more than someone who develops diabetes, they are only responsible for sorting out what, for them, is the best way of handling it.

Cognitive avoidance is an intrinsic part of PTSD and because of this the client is likely to be highly anxious about disclosing the trauma to the counsellor and even more so to other group members. It is therefore important to stress that the prime focus of the group is teaching members how to handle the memories that intrude anyway and that any disclosure is entirely in the hands of the client. A related issue is that of secondary traumatization, a fear that hearing of others' traumas will retraumatize them. This can be addressed by telling them that victims of trauma like themselves do not like talking about their trauma and that therefore they would only hear of others' traumas in such measured doses that it would not overwhelm them.

A further problem in engaging some PTSD clients is the issue of safety. In some instances their assailant is perhaps out on bail or intimidating the client, perhaps through a third party. In other instances the assailant has served a prison sentence because of the attack and is back in the client's locality. The issue of client safety is paramount and in a few instances it is not possible to proceed with a programme until the threat recedes.

It can also be more difficult to engage a PTSD client in a programme when it is five years or more since the trauma. At this stage it is often the depression symptoms and relationship difficulties that are uppermost in their mind, having reached a new equilibrium with the trauma. But it is likely to be an unhealthy equilibrium, fuelling their inter- and intrapersonal problems. Their PTSD can be likened to someone with a back injury initially unable to walk who then, with the help of a walking stick, manages to get about a bit. The question is whether they want a back operation and the attendant initial discomfort (the treatment programme) to enable them to function much as before their trauma, or whether are they going to be content to continue to hobble about with a stick.

Some chronic PTSD clients are best advised not to make a decision about a programme immediately but to go away and think it over and get back to the counsellor if they wish to avail themselves of it. It should be stressed however that the evidence to date (Kessler *et al.* 1996) on the natural history of PTSD suggests that it is very unlikely that at this stage there would be any naturally occurring improvement in their condition. However, giving these clients time to make a decision results in a more stable decision and may help prevent premature disengagement from the group, which is disquieting not only for the individual but for other group members.

TARGETS

The goals of the group are:

1. to help clients interact adaptively with their memory of the trauma;
2. to test out their beliefs on the dangerousness of ordinary situations;
3. to restore connections with those in their personal world;
4. to adapt or reinstate pre-trauma goals.

FORMAT OF 10 SESSION GROUP AND INDIVIDUAL PROGRAMME FOR PTSD

Session One. Introductions and Handling the Trauma Memory

The programme begins, as do all the group programmes, by stressing the need for confidentiality. Some members of a group PTSD programme may require simultaneous individual sessions if there is substantial trauma-related guilt that they are unable to address in the group, for example if they were the perpetrator of a crime or if the trauma has reawakened feelings associated with childhood physical or sexual abuse.

The availability of such sessions should be made known at the outset. In any one group probably only one or two members will avail themselves of this. The refreshment break at the end of each session provides a setting for determining the appropriateness of such an arrangement. In addition an individual session is required between the first and second group session to troubleshoot any problems with the group format and ensure engagement with the memory of the trauma.

Clients with PTSD have lost a sense of who they are, and the development of a coherent and historically consistent sense of self is an important therapeutic goal. A first step in the reconstruction process is to ask each member of the group to get to know the person next to them for 10 minutes. Each member then has the task of introducing their partner to the group. The instructions to participants for this exercise are deliberately vague, with no indication given of whether they mention their trauma or not, but the implication is that they are not just defined by their trauma experience.

The feedback to the group at large may however indicate the degree of cognitive avoidance of the trauma by particular clients and this should be noted by the group leaders. This exercise can build group cohesion if leaders can underline some similarities of, say, interests, work experience or family arrangements. Spending some time on these non-trauma related issues makes the group members feel safe and makes manifest defining characteristics of their current identity other than as trauma victims. When several clients have declared information about their trauma the leaders should again point to similarities in either the objective nature of the trauma, e.g. two members have experienced motor vehicle accidents, or the subjective similarities, e.g. some thought that they were going to die, all showed feelings of helplessness. Those who have disclosed aspects of the trauma to the group act as important models for those yet to disclose.

In instances where clients are only disclosing the trauma the leaders should seek elaboration of the non-trauma related self, again by implication saying that they are more than their trauma. This can be encapsulated by the leaders saying that the client is not just a victim or, better, a survivor, but a whole person with a history.

The format of the introductions section of this first session provides a backcloth to the main theoretical rationale for the programme, which is that individuals are able to cope with an extreme trauma to the extent that they are able to take account of the trauma whilst simultaneously elaborating on their pre-trauma experiences of their personal world and produce a benign, integrated story of their life.

The second major topic covered in this session is handling the memory of the trauma. Before describing to group members new ways of handling the trauma memory it is necessary that they come to an understanding of the futility of their current coping strategy. To do this the leaders should go round the group and elicit each individual's coping strategies and list them on a board. The coping strategies almost always involve cognitive and/or emotional avoidance. Some commonly elicited strategies are given in Figure 6.4.

The next step is to enquire whether the strategies work and, if so, for how long? Most clients readily agree that the avoidance only works briefly and the trauma memory soon returns. The group leaders can amplify this as follows.

TYPICAL COPING STRATEGIES

Go and make a drink

Go for a walk

Get into a conversation with someone about something else

Do something in the garden

Avoid the spot where the incident occurred

Drink to forget

Figure 6.4   Typical Strategies for Coping with Intrusive Memories in PTSD

Leader. Trauma memories are, as it were, on an elastic band – the more you push them away the harder they spring back and you get more injured in the end. Ultimately the band snaps and you snap at yourself and others. At this point you get lost in the details of the trauma, e.g. the smell of the dead body, eyes like a cod. It is then like disappearing down a 'black hole', the memory is controlling you rather than you controlling the memory. Your waking and sleeping hours are controlled by the memory. You pay a very heavy price for trying to block the memory. On the other hand you understandably do not want it to dominate your life. There is however a better way of handling the trauma memory.

Co-leader. The key is to regard the trauma memory a bit like a local thug, perhaps a bully you can remember from your schooldays. It is not very bright to totally ignore or become aggressive with the thug. You may have developed the skill of exchanging pleasantries with him but you take care not to get involved with him. You perhaps learnt to develop a matter-of-fact style in the face of this potential adversary so that life could go on. In a similar way when people have experienced extreme trauma they have to cultivate such a style, but it takes practice and, initially at least, you will still feel uncomfortable. To begin with it will be a question of coping with the memory rather than mastering the memory.

Group members are then introduced to the specifics of interacting adaptively with the memory of the trauma by reading through and discussing Items (1) and (2) on the Managing PTSD handout of Figure 6.5.

MANAGING POSTTRAUMATIC STRESS DISORDER

1. MANAGING THE MEMORY
If you try to block out the memory of the incident you will find that it does not really work, it keeps coming back. To help you control the memory rather than have the memory control you, each time the memory comes to mind say to yourself 'Now is not the time and place. I will sort that out properly with pen and paper at [say] 11a.m. when I will write down whatever I can manage about what happened and how I felt.' Spending a couple of minutes at a fixed time writing about it (or talking about it to someone) tells your mind that you are in charge of the memory and it acts as a safety valve for the memory otherwise it is all bottled up inside you and you feel ready to explode. The first days of writing about it can be very upsetting so you might just do a minute or two to begin with. As the days go on it gets easier and after two or three weeks you will find the memory does not get to you in the way it used to.

2. 'YES . . ., BUT . . .' THE MEMORY
With posttraumatic stress disorder people get sucked into the details of the incident like a 'black hole' that can swallow you up and stop ordinary living. When a detail of the incident comes to mind, calmly acknowledge the horror of the details '**Yes** it was horrible that . . .' and then put the horror into context '**but** the incident was a one-off, nothing like it had ever happened to me before, I have had many more positive experiences in life that tell me life can be good'.

3. UNLOCK POSITIVE MEMORIES
With posttraumatic stress disorder positive memories are locked away in your mind, you know they are there but they are vague. To make the positives come alive spend a couple of minutes each day going into great detail about two particular events, e.g. a holiday or the birth of a child. Either write or talk about them.

4. TIMETABLE UPLIFTS
Timetable into your week things that could be potentially uplifting. Have a go at them even if you don't feel like it. If you keep active eventually the taste for life comes back. To begin with you might have to do things in small doses, e.g. visit a friend for twenty minutes for a coffee rather than stay all evening. The timetable is a way of reminding yourself that despite the disruption caused by the incident it is possible to get a sense of achievement and pleasure out of life, though what you now do might be different to before.

5. MANAGING IRRITABILITY
When you notice the first signs of anger imagine a set of traffic lights on red and shout 'STOP!' to yourself. As the lights go to amber ask yourself 'Am I absolutely sure they did that to deliberately wind me up? Is it really the end of the world that [X] has just happened?' When the lights go to green go into another room to calm down, or perhaps make a hot drink.

Figure 6.5 Managing Posttraumatic Stress Disorder Handout

The first item on the handout can be introduced by continuing the school bully analogy.

Leader. It is as if you have reached the limits of your tolerance with the school bully and you have agreed to see him at a certain time and place. Avoiding him has meant that your life had become very restricted. You have considerable misgivings, however, about the wisdom of such a meeting even though you know it is the only way you can move forward. But in writing about your trauma you are now taking control – you choose the time and duration. It does not matter if you begin with just a sentence a day.

Though Item (1) on the handout seems straightforward, cognitive avoidance can occur in a number of guises. The trauma may be reported rather like a police report with little of the idiosyncratic thought processes or the emotions specified. To counter this, clients are asked to write their account in the first person, 'I am lying on the motorway . . .'. Sometimes the avoidance takes the form of writing a diary of how the incident has affected them. The leaders should anticipate these forms of avoidance by ruling them out in advance of setting Item (1) as a homework exercise. The incident has first to be acknowledged in order to be subsequently contextualized. Clients' engagement with the trauma memory is such a crucial and painful issue that an individual session should be arranged between the first and second group sessions in order to review this interaction.

Item (2) on the handout, the 'Yes . . . , But . . .' strategy, can be introduced along the following lines.

Leader. PTSD symptoms are often experienced like a wave of terror coming over you. To begin with you will not be able to stop the waves coming, if you try to you will just get more frustrated. Do not try to pretend that the terror has not come, do not get cross with yourself for its arrival, you are not responsible for its visit, but you have to say 'Yes' to the visitor, acknowledge it as calmly as possible, accept the physical sensations, the images, whilst acknowledging their full horror. You must properly say 'Yes' before 'Butting' the memory and putting the visitor in its place. There are usually two aspects to a 'Yes . . ., But . . .'. The first is another angle on the incident itself. For instance you might move from saying 'I was driving. There was blood on my friend after we were hit. I hurt her' to 'Yes my friend was hurt. But I did not assault her.' The second 'Yes . . ., But . . .' puts the incident into the context of your life and locates it to a specific time and place and makes the point that it only has relevance in that unique situation, i.e. it is not typical of life. Say 'Yes, that was an awful experience. I would not wish it on my worst enemy. But it was on March 10th 1996 at 9.50 p.m. It belongs then. It was totally different to anything before and is almost certainly a once in a lifetime experience. I will see it as having visited Hell, but the good news is I have returned' It is very important not to expect too much of the 'Yes . . ., Buts . . .', certainly initially. At most they will to begin with take the edge off the sensations you experience. With practice and probably some gradual alteration of your particular 'Yes . . ., But . . .' they percolate down in the words of the TV advert 'to the parts that other strategies cannot reach' and you begin to feel real change. But it is a percolation process you cannot hurry.

This should be followed by asking the group whether they already use any 'Yes . . ., Buts . . .'.

Ian. Yes, I try and tell myself 'Yes but my accident could have been much worse, the road is usually much busier, with schoolchildren crossing' but that just gets me really wound up when I think of the possible carnage.

Leader. The right 'Yes . . ., But . . .' is one that leaves you less distressed. Yours, Ian, is making it worse. Your mind is going dancing and playing a catastrophic video and it is no wonder you feel distressed. What we have got to get you to do is to play a reality video.

Ian. What, you mean like concentrating on the fact that I survived?

Leader. Yes, perhaps your 'Yes . . ., But . . .' should be in two parts. First 'Yes, the incident was awful. But I have survived' and then 'Yes, I can still remember the feelings of helplessness as the cab went towards the house. But nothing else like it has happened in twenty years driving. It was a one off.'

Ian. It makes me sweat when I think of the helplessness.

Co-leader. We can't wipe away those initial physiological reactions but what we can do is to help you put them in their place.

John. But Ian's right isn't he? Someone could have died. You can't just forget that. As you know that child did die when I was driving the Heavy Goods Vehicle.

Leader. You have a point, John. We can't dismiss the possibility of an extreme outcome, but extreme outcomes are extremely unlikely.

You can only live in the present by playing a reality video of the most likely sequence of events, i.e. the sequence of events that you would put money on happening. If you play catastrophic videos we would not continue to sit under this ceiling because it is possible that it might fall in.

Co-leader. Horrible traumas can give you a mistaken impression of how likely an incident is. If you have someone living next door who you see die of some horrible rare disease you might start to inspect yourself for signs afterwards. It is understandable but finally you have to stop the checking and calmly remind yourself of how rare it is and that there is no reason to believe that you should be singled out as especially vulnerable any more than the rest of the human race.

Individual Session (Core). Locking on to the Trauma Memory

Up to the point of entering the programme, clients' interactions with the memory of their traumas will have been automatic, a fight or flight response. The suggestion that they stay with the memory long enough to contextualize it is likely to evoke fears that they will be over-whelmed. Consequently their feelings of being unsafe are likely to have been heightened at the start of the programme. It is therefore recommended that an individual session is scheduled after the first group session.

In this session the counsellor should be aware of the contrast between what the client has written about the trauma and their verbal description of the trauma elicited at the first assessment session. It is important that the counsellor has to hand an almost verbatim copy of what the client said at the assessment, together with the counsellor's notes of any particularly strong emotions evoked at any point in the proceedings or any physiological reaction such as sweating. The client's initial description of both the objective and subjective aspects of their trauma will typically have taken at least 15 minutes to elaborate.

The client should first of all be congratulated on anything that they have written and praised for attempting to engage with the material. What the client has written should be read back by the counsellor who should pause at any point where the client gets markedly distressed.

At such points of intensification of emotion the counsellor asks 'What was going through your mind there that caused you to get upset?' In this way the counsellor is able to identify the core of the client's distress. Clients have usually left something out of their written account and in some instances may not have written anything. The client is then asked why they left out various aspects that were obviously 'hot' for them at the initial assessment. In this way the client is engaged in elaborating in turn on various aspects of the trauma, e.g. 'You were saying at the initial interview that sometimes as you are going to sleep you get a picture of yourself lying face down on the motorway, and you have to open your eyes because you can not bear what you see. What do you see, the car coming over your leg?'

In the second half of the interview the client is encouraged to add to what they have written. Where a client has been unable to write anything, the counsellor has to take over the job of authorship. The writing has to be done as if the client were giving the account of the trauma, seeking the client's approval for every sentence – 'Have I got that right? Have I missed the point? Is there something that I have missed out?' The aim is to have, by the end of the session, an account of the trauma of about 150 words in the client's terminology which is reasonably comprehensive – the client's story of the event. Such an account should take no more than about 90 seconds to read through. The client is then set for homework the task of modifying or changing what is written to produce another 90 second version that they would be prepared to read out at the next group session to 'put other group members in the picture', emphasizing that they are in control of what, if anything, they will read out. They are free to present an expurgated or unexpurgated version of their trauma at the next session. Fears of doing this can be assuaged by noting that 'Everybody will be in the same boat.'

An alternative strategy to use when the client has been unable to write anything is a technique described by Ochberg (1996). The client is asked to gaze at some fixed point in the room and then to remember the various aspects of the trauma – without verbalizing them – as the counsellor counts from 1 to 100. They are advised to focus on less distressing aspects of the trauma when the count is around 20–30, reaching the worst parts with the count around 50, then back to less distressing parts of the memory as the end of the count approaches. At around 90 the counsellor says 'Back here' to help bring the client back to the present. Afterwards the client is asked what went through their mind, and usually gives a comprehensive account of the trauma. The counsellor can then write down this account, checking the details with the client, and this becomes the client's story.

However, some clients' cognitive avoidance is so great that they cannot even verbalize their trauma. Using the Ochberg technique it is possible to overcome this by asking, for example, 'What was going through your mind at 20–30?' or at even earlier points in the count, thereby gaining entry to the client's trauma.

When clients are insistent that they could not tell the group about the trauma the counsellor should then endeavour to make an audiotape of their trauma from the account given, lasting perhaps two to three minutes. They are then asked for homework to 'bore' themselves with (i.e. desensitize themselves to) the memory, using the Trauma Tape form (Figure 6.6), stressing that they should eschew rumination and postpone consideration of the trauma to the daily time for listening to the tape.

What the Ochberg technique and the counsellor recorded trauma tape have in common is that they render it safer for the client to address the memory of the trauma by linking the therapist's voice to the account of the trauma. The fundamental message to be conveyed by this session is that the counsellor can provide the client with sufficient safety within which to address the trauma.

At this individual session it is also important to elicit feedback on their initial experience of the group and to troubleshoot any diffi-culties. Similarities between the client and other group members in terms of the objective trauma, their subjective response to the trauma or difficulties in reconnecting with people and engaging with life should be emphasized in the interests of developing group cohesion. This cohesion is important in all the group programmes described in this volume but it is especially important with chronic PTSD clients who have often been unable to properly communicate their experi-ence to anyone and whose often antisocial behaviour has led to a very solitary existence. Their membership of the group testifies that they still 'belong' in a way that purely individual counselling for the con-dition cannot.

TRAUMA TAPE

Play the trauma tape each day. It is easier to get around to listening to it if you decide in advance on a particular time, say 11.00 am (do not play it anywhere near bedtime). At the end of each playthrough, before you rewind it, write down a number 0 to 10 in the table below that describes how you are feeling: 0 is feeling very low, 3 would be pretty low, 5 is so-so, 7 pretty good, and a 10 would be feeling superb.
Play the tape over and over for about 15 minutes. Only finish with it when you are not feeling too low.

Week 1	Mon	Tue	Wed	Thur	Fri	Sat	Sun
1							
2							
3							
4							
5							
6							
7							
8							
9							
10							

Week 2	Mon	Tue	Wed	Thur	Fri	Sat	Sun
1							
2							
3							
4							
5							
6							
7							
8							
9							
10							

Week 3	Mon	Tue	Wed	Thur	Fri	Sat	Sun
1							
2							
3							
4							
5							
6							
7							
8							
9							
10							

Figure 6.6   Trauma Tape

Session Two (Core). Review of Revisiting the Trauma and Review of 'Yes . . . , Buts . . .'

This session begins with the leader inviting members to tell their trauma story from what they have written 'for just a minute or so', inviting first of all someone who seemed least disturbed at the individual session in the construction of their narrative. In this way a process of telling their trauma rather than reliving the experience is modelled for other, perhaps more distressed, group members. After each narrative is read out (those who do not feel comfortable enough even after gentle encouragement to read their transcript are allowed not to do so) the story is discussed in the group for about 10 minutes. The leaders begin the discussion by thanking the person for sharing it, using some metaphor that highlights the importance of trying to verbalize the experience.

Co-leader. Thanks for that Ian, it is often difficult to begin to put into words the horror, but if you can name the enemy – the memory, the feelings – you can begin to deal with it. It's been stuck in your throat for years stopping you swallowing life and you're beginning to get it up. Unless you have a safety valve for the release of the memory it all builds up inside and you feel that you are going to explode. This is why probably most of the group are having 'explosions' with friends and family, there is a need for a safety valve.

This thanking should take place through any sobs of distress of the client legitimating that distress but at the same time underlining the fact that they have taken an all-important first step along the road to recovery.

The discussion of the narrative is begun gently by the leaders locating the incident in time and place then leaving space for other group members to comment. Their initial comments usually reflect an identification with the narrator's subjective response to the incident, validating their own experience. This is often followed by a challenge to the client's interpretation of the trauma.

Ian. What do you mean, John, you should have been going slower? You were only going 30–40 mph.

John. But if I had maybe the driver of the other vehicle would not have
  been killed.
Ian. If you had driven any slower at rush hour you would have caused
  another accident before it. I know I get frustrated with slow drivers.

In the above extract Ian attempted to switch John from a primarily
perceptual processing of the trauma, namely that the driver of an
oncoming car that was overtaking another vehicle was killed, to a
more abstract conceptual level. The co-leader was able to build on
this.

Co-leader. That sounds like a 'Yes . . ., But . . .'; 'Yes it was tragic that
  the other driver died, my guts wrench when I think about it. But if I
  had been driving any slower I may have caused an accident earlier.'
  Would you be able to try out that 'Yes . . ., But . . .' when these
  waves of feelings hit you, John?
John. I will give anything a try.

The second part of this session is a review of the practice of 'Yes . . .,
Buts . . .'.

Ian. Sometimes the 'Yes . . ., But . . .' seemed to work but sometimes
  the situation took over. My worst one was somebody stopping
  sharply at a junction. I became so angry that I had to stop the car and
  get myself together. Then I felt stupid because there was no real
  danger. So I am only making absolutely essential journeys.
Leader. To begin with it can be a fair bit after the event that you come
  up with a 'Yes . . ., But . . .'. At the start you have to really con-
  sciously spell out the 'Yes . . ., Buts . . .' then with practice they
  become almost automatic and nip your distress in the bud. So con-
  gratulate yourself Ian for coming up with your 'Yes . . ., But . . .';
  'Yes it is frightening when cars are approaching from a side road.
  But I do know that I am safe'. It is rather like learning to drive a car,
  first of all you have to really spell out what you have to do. Then
  after a time you can do it without thinking.

This exchange highlights the intended switch from deliberate, effortful
processing, operating at a declarative level with the 'Yes . . ., Buts . . .',
to an increasingly automated procedural processing at a pre-conscious
level. It is this latter which will more likely influence the initial
physiological response to an alarming situation.

Sessions Three and Four. Review of Earlier Sessions and Contrasting the Trauma with Previous Life Experiences by Contextualizing Rules for Living Then and Now

These sessions begin with a review of the rewritten stories, then the focus moves to an account of a typical week before the trauma, presented as a 'getting to know each other more fully' exercise. The idea of the latter is to build a bridge over the trauma, access the former self and its *modus operandi*. Then, in the interactions with other group members, to provide a corrective emotional experience which 'draws across the bridge' former ways of operating and rules for living that enhance the quality of life. In these sessions the dual focus on the trauma and pre-trauma experiences mirrors the necessary contextualizing of the trauma.

In their rewritten scenarios clients often introduce material that has not been presented before and this should be focused on by one of the group leaders.

Co-leader. That's new Ian, I didn't know that someone had been standing in the pub doorway as you went towards it.
Ian. Yes, I can still see the look of horror on his face as he saw me approaching as if it was yesterday.
Co-leader. Was he injured?
Ian. No, he got inside pretty damn quick, but when I think of what could have happened to him I go sick.

Here again the client's account of the trauma is staying at a perceptual level, 'the sight', the somatic response 'sick'. The therapeutic goal is to transform it to a conceptual level.

Leader. If the man in the doorway was present here now what do you think he would be saying of the experience?
Ian. Scary!
Leader. Do you think he would be worrying about the incident?
Ian. No, he was OK.
Leader. He might be saying, 'Yes, it was scary for a moment. But there was no real danger to me.'
Ian. I could borrow his 'Yes . . ., But . . .'.
Leader. If you like. Try it on for size, see if it fits.

Group members are asked to rewrite their trauma scripts again for presentation at the next session.

The leaders next need to ask group members in turn to describe a typical week before the trauma. It is important to get group members to be as specific as possible about their pre-trauma experiences, hence the focus on a typical week. Most clients with PTSD, left to their own devices, speak of their pre-trauma, days in generalities, e.g. 'I was happy then' or alternatively 'Life has always been a pain' and compare it with their current difficulties in relating to others and the world expressed in more specific terms, e.g., 'We drove to Wales last week-end heading for the Falls. I got a bit lost, threw a tantrum, gave up and came home. What a waste. It was not fair on my wife.' The task of the leaders is to help group members stay sufficiently in the pre-trauma experiences to elaborate on the taken-for-granted assumptions that underpinned that behaviour and to distil what pre-trauma coping strategies might be salvaged. The following extract demonstrates the approach.

Leader. What was a typical week for you, Sarah, before you were attacked in the Off Licence?

Sarah. I used to go to a pub or the Taxi Club a couple of times a week. But I have not bothered to renew my membership of the Club, I haven't the time for people now.

Leader. So you used to enjoy being with people?

Sarah. Oh yes, my husband used to complain that he could not take me anywhere without my knowing someone. I used to love nothing better than a good chat.

Leader. Do you think that the people you used to chat to have changed?

Sarah. No, it's me.

Co-leader. What is it about you that's changed?

Sarah. Everything. I am not the same person.

Co-leader. Is that really true? You have still got red hair. Maybe the only real difference is that you are afraid?

Sarah. You are right. I will not go out by myself because I think my assailant will harm me.

Co-leader. But he wore a mask, didn't he?

Sarah. I just see those eyes peering out. It makes me shudder.

Co-leader. But why should he seek you out and want to harm you?

Sarah. The police said from the route he took and other robberies in the area he probably lives locally.

John. But why should he have a go at you Sarah? I would have thought he would want to stay well out of your way.

Sarah. I just feel vulnerable.

Leader. You had worked as manageress of the Off Licence for 10 years before, hadn't you Sarah? Did you go to work expecting to be safe?

Sarah. Oh yes, I had some good times.

Leader. So your belief that you were safe worked, it paid off?

Sarah. Maybe I was just lucky.

Leader. What, lucky on something like 3000 days?

Sarah. I see what you mean.

Leader. If you were able to tell yourself what you took for granted before the incident, that you could expect to be safe going out that day, maybe you could begin to enjoy people's company again.

Sarah. Maybe, but then there are these panic attacks every time I try and go out by myself.

Leader. Can we discuss your handling of them over coffee at the end and we might also need to build in an individual session or two to address them?

Sarah. That is fine.

At the end of the above exchange the client mentions a common co-morbid problem – panic disorder. If more than one member of the group has such a disorder then the group leaders can more easily legitimate some time in the session devoted to the issue. However if, as is often the case, only one person is affected it is better dealt with using the above strategy of scheduling in an additional individual session.

Sometimes clients have done something during the traumatic event that made the outcome less awful than it might otherwise have been. The client's attention should be drawn to this to assist in reducing the sense of helplessness evoked by the trauma memory.

Leader. Sarah, you mentioned that you struggled not to be pushed back into the shop by your assailant. Your fear was that once inside the shop he would try and open the safe, would not believe you when you told him it was on a timelock, and in his frustration would have killed you with his knife. In the event you stopped him from pushing you back through the door. You did well there. Even in that extreme situation you were able to make a difference. Has anyone else managed to influence things in that sort of way?

Mary. Yes, I did wake up my sister and the other hotel residents when the fire broke out. I thought that we weren't going to get out but we did.

Co-leader. The fire occurred at about 1.00 a.m. when most of the residents were asleep, is that right?

Mary. Yes.

Sarah. God, if you had not done that they would have died.

Mary. I only did what I had to.

Leader. Yes, but you made a difference to the traumatic event, you did influence things. In some situations like those of Ian and John it was impossible to influence the event, but in yours, Mary and Sarah, you did.

Mary. I guess so.

Sometimes, however, it is an exaggerated sense of control that is at the heart of a client's trauma-related guilt. For example a rape victim might blame herself for walking down an isolated lane and this guilt needs to be addressed. One approach to this is to enquire whether it was reasonably foreseeable in this case, whether a significant proportion of women would have walked down that lane at the time. The strategy is then to suggest that it was not unreasonable at the time. This focus on the constraints and circumstances existing at the time of the trauma is crucial to the client assuaging themselves of trauma-related guilt. Confronted with a trauma many clients freeze or rush to perform an action that in retrospect was not the best option. In the case of frenzied activity oxygen has to be pumped to the large muscles in order to take action, depriving oneself of the composure needed for a carefully thought-out response.

Mary. I tried desperately to revive the old lady who had fallen asleep in the lounge, but I think I just should have pulled her out instead.

Co-leader. But how do you know that if you had pulled her out and then tried to revive her she wouldn't have died anyway?

Mary. I don't, but I just feel so guilty.

Ian. I don't think the lady would be blaming you.

Mary. I know, but that's not the point.

Co-leader. What is the point?

Mary. I feel incredibly guilty.

Leader. Maybe all we can do is alter your reaction to those guilt feelings rather than try and take them away. Treat them as a mental cold, uncomfortable, but not to be taken too seriously. A 'Yes . . . I do feel

extremely uncomfortable with these guilt feelings. But I do not have
to buy into them, I can carry them, acknowledge them.'

Mary. I wish I could, but next weekend is the second anniversary.

Leader. But you can 'Yes . . ., But . . .' that day. 'Yes, March 26th can be
a horrendous day if I remember the fire. But it could also be a really
good day to remember if, say, I took a weekend flight to Monte
Carlo!' You can re-write history.

Mary. Monte Carlo!! Will you pay? Coming with me Sarah?

Co-leader. It's just making sure the trauma memory doesn't have the
last word.

These sessions finish by asking clients not only to re-write the script
of their trauma, but also, and separately, to spend ten to fifteen minutes each day writing about positive experiences from their pre-
trauma life.

Sessions Five and Six. Reconnecting with Others and Establishing Goals

The close relationships of PTSD clients are inevitably strained and they
are often goalless. These sessions get under way, as always, with a
review of the homework assignments.

Co-leader. Can anyone tell us about some positive incident from before
the trauma?

John. Yes, I wrote about the Liverpool v Newcastle game, it was an
absolute classic. Liverpool won 4–3 in the end. When I was writing
about it I felt more my old self than for ages.

Co-leader. But that's not your old self John, that is you. The you who is
sensible enough to be a Liverpool supporter rather than an Everton
supporter!

Ian. Steady on!

John. Been a Liverpool supporter since I went to the match with my
Dad as a child.

Co-leader. Ah! A Liverpool supporter through and through. But that
says as much about you and your life as ever the trauma does.

John. I know, I just feel sick still when the incident comes to mind.

Sarah. But there's more to you than that accident, John. I reckon you're
a big softy.

John. What?

Mary. That's a compliment.
Leader. Think about it, John.

Relating and juxtaposing trauma and pre-trauma experiences both for homework and in the session provides the means for contextualizing the trauma.

Close relationships are strained by the development of uncharacteristic irritability, emotional numbness and avoidance of activities. The uncharacteristic irritability often has its basis in the PTSD client's perceived inability to perform a previously valued role, but this frustration is often expressed in the context of very minor hassles, e.g. one's partner forgetting to buy bread. The over-reaction to minor inconveniences begets an over-reaction from the partner, and escalates into arguments. These conflicts are rarely resolved because they are not really about the ostensible subject matter. Over time, partners often cope by distancing themselves from each other. In turn this enhances the PTSD client's feeling that 'Nobody understands' and sometimes leads to taking solace in drink or drugs – with the partner increasingly looking to other relationships for support.

A particular problem is posed by the emotional numbness or emptiness of the PTSD client. Because many PTSD clients are leading a hermit-like existence, making excuses to avoid previous friends and family, they can easily conclude that their lack of a positive emotional response to their partner is a sign that they are no longer in love with their partner. These feelings may become the client's guilty secret, resulting in debilitation or, if expressed, leading to further estrangement from the partner. An additional source of strain is that the PTSD client is spending more time with their partner since the trauma, but is almost wholly inactive, to the former's chagrin or annoyance. It is therefore necessary to help the PTSD client elaborate clear and manageable life goals.

It is usually a good sign of progress in PTSD clients if they become able to talk with their partner or significant other about the trauma. The verbalizing of the trauma requires a labelling of confusing emotions but the client thereby attains a measure of control. (In cases where the PTSD client is unable to write about the trauma this can be used as a substitute). But communication between the PTSD client and partner is often impeded by the former's insistence that the latter completely comprehend their trauma, and as soon as it becomes apparent that there is less than total understanding communication is halted. This can be particularly frustrating to a partner who believes that hitherto they had good communication. Part of these sessions should be devoted to encouraging group members to talk about the trauma to their partner for just a couple of minutes each day. It has to be stressed that their partner will only accept discussion of the trauma for a limited period each day, because to do otherwise would represent a failure to contextualize the experience, that is it would relegate in importance all their joint, positive, pre-trauma interactions, such as cycling with their children in the local park. The emphasis should be on partners' committing themselves to trying to understand each other, rather than expecting instant attainment of that understanding.

Reconnection is also a major issue for single PTSD clients who may have been physically scarred by their trauma or lost a limb. Usually there is at most one member in a PTSD group for whom adapting to disfigurement or disability is a major issue and it is not therefore easy or appropriate to tackle it in the group. These aspects are often better addressed in an interpolated individual session. On the one hand these clients often desperately want to be in a relationship where they are special to someone, but the thought of rejection is terrifying and the prospect of the discovery of their scarring in a sexual relationship mortifying. It is useful to give such clients the last two chapters of Simon Weston's autobiography, *Walking Tall* (Weston, 1989). He was badly facially disfigured in the Falklands War, and the final chapters 'Looking Back' and 'Looking On', provide a commendable model of successful adaptation. For example he reframes the concerns of many unattached people with such disabilities about whether they will meet someone special, by advising that at least if they do meet such a person they will know that it is not a superficial relationship and will last.

Not only PTSD clients with disabilities or disfigurements but virtually all PTSD clients have to establish new goals. Often a major obstacle to the elaboration and pursuit of a new goal is the client's belief that they should not have to redirect their energies, they have been the hapless victims of fate. The group leader's task is to acknowledge these feelings, i.e. help the client say 'Yes' to them, and then to ask pragmatically 'But does it work, saying that it's not fair?' It is recommended that clients are asked to construct a 'mental video' of themselves saying 'It's all not fair' and then to decide whether the watching of such a video is helpful in the long term.

Clients can be particularly reluctant to change track if their pre-trauma role was overvalued, i.e. the role was perceived as the sole gateway to self-efficacy – a sense of achievement and pleasure. In the work context such clients can be introduced to the notion that perhaps they were addicted to their organization, i.e. they behaved as if there was no life beyond the organization, and that therapy is partly about weaning them off their employer, with associated withdrawal symptoms. Possible new goals should be tackled in an experimental fashion, adopting a 'you don't know until you try' approach. Because the average PTSD client is moderately depressed it is important that any goal is broken down into small manageable steps, with breaks in between before progressing to the next sub-goal.

Sessions Seven to Nine. Understanding the Information Conveyed by Emotions, Errors of Interpretation and the Challenging of Safety Beliefs

The previous sessions have focused on PTSD clients reconnecting with others. One of the hidden obstacles to this is often the client's lack of understanding of their own emotional response. For example, emotional numbness is a common symptom of PTSD, yet few clients directly attribute this to their trauma. Because their lives typically become circumscribed they can easily connect this lack of affect to their partner, concluding that they are no longer in love with them, leading to the breakdown of probably their most salient relationship. More generally, the PTSD client attempts to justify their emotional state in terms of something in the present, thus their fear response might be justified by news of some horror in the media.

There is a variety of cognitive processes that can be used to justify a sense of continuing threat and these are examined in these sessions. Figure 6.7 (from Scott and Stradling, 1992, p. 43) lists some typical errors of information processing post trauma, and these same processes can be operative in the interpretation of the trauma itself.

ERRORS OF INFORMATION PROCESSING IN PTSD

1. *All or nothing thinking*. Everything is seen in black-and-white terms, for example 'I am either in control of what's happening to me or I am not'.

2. *Over-generalization*. Expecting a uniform response from a category of people because of the misdeeds of a member, for example 'All men are potential rapists'.

3. *Mental filter*. Seizing on a negative fragment of a situation and dwelling on it, for example 'I could have been killed in that encounter'.

4. *Automatic discounting*. Brushing aside the positive aspects of what was achieved in a trauma, for example 'I was only doing my duty in saving the child'.

5. *Jumping to conclusions*. Assuming that it is known what others think, for example 'They all think I should be over it now, it was six months ago after all'.

6. *Magnification and minimization*. Magnification of shortcomings and minimization of strengths, for example 'Since the trauma I am so irritable with the family and just about manage to keep going to work'.

7. *Emotional reasoning*. Focusing on emotional state to draw conclusions about oneself, for example 'Since it happened, I am frightened of my own shadow, I guess I am just a wimp'.

8. *'Should' statements*. Inappropriate use of moral imperatives – 'shoulds', 'musts', 'haves', and 'oughts' – for example 'It's ridiculous that since the attack I now have to take my daughter shopping with me. I should be able to go by myself.'

9. *Labelling and mislabelling*. For example 'I used to think of myself as a strong person. I could handle anything, but since it happened I am just weak.'

10. *Personalization*. Assuming that because something went wrong it must be your fault. 'I keep going over my handling of the situation. I must have made a mistake somewhere for the child to have died.'

Figure 6.7   Errors of Information Processing in PTSD

Thus the client justifying their fearfulness in terms of a news item in the media would be using a mental filter. The leaders should discuss each of these errors of processing, inviting group members to volunteer examples, and write down ones pertinent to themselves. There are no watertight distinctions between the ten thought processes, and any one client is likely to habitually use a particular two or three. Once clients become aware of their propensity for specific errors, they can use them as an immediate fault-finding list to help them stand back and critically assess their distress at any point in time. For homework, group members are asked to monitor their mood, noting the time, place and context of any down-turn in mood, then to perform a slow motion 'action replay' of the changes, scrutinizing them for any errors of processing, then to write down a more realistic way of thinking about the situation.

The key cognitive shift sought in these sessions is to have the client attribute their negative emotions to the past rather than the present. This can be illustrated to group members by referring to the film *Ryan's Daughter* in which a soldier is on leave from the battles in the trenches of the First World War. He goes into a pub in an idyllic little village in the West of Ireland and stands at the bar. The pub is empty except for a barmaid collecting glasses. She drops the tray with a crash and he curls up in a ball on the floor, experiencing intense flashbacks of being back in the trenches. As time goes on he is better able to check his fear reaction, reminding himself that he is in the West of Ireland. Implicitly he was putting a particular time and place label on his uncomfortable 'gut reactions'. Successful processing of emotional information requires that the client learn to stop and think through the meaning of an emotion rather than engage in a 'knee-jerk' reflex reaction.

Simply making PTSD clients aware that they are getting faulty signals, 'false alarms', from their body is of itself insufficient for a re-engagement in pre-trauma like activities; they have to be encouraged to collect data that would contradict the messages from their body. An analogy can help make this point.

Leader. If you were in a friend's car and you noticed that the fuel gauge was indicating empty, you would probably be alarmed. If your friend said 'It is probably a faulty gauge', this would probably not reassure you. What would really convince you that it was a faulty gauge would be if you then drove a great distance without any problems. To reach the parts that matter you need action.

For homework clients are asked to challenge safety beliefs that they have been operating on since the trauma e.g., 'I am only safe if I go to the pub when it is empty.' These beliefs should be explicated in the sessions and the actions that would constitute a contradiction of them agreed for practice.

Sarah. I burst out crying for no reason at work. I feel stupid, the smallest hassle sets me off.

Leader. Does that happen at home?

Sarah. No, if I am at home and have got my family around me I am fine, but outside I am struggling. The other day my husband could not pick me up from work and he arranged for my daughter to collect me. She was 15 minutes late and I was in an awful state when she arrived.

Leader. You play 'horror videos' when you are anywhere other than home?

Sarah. When I rang home and did not get any answer I was beside myself.

Co-leader. What was in your horror movie?

Sarah. I thought 'Something's happened to my husband, nobody's coming for me, I am trapped'.

Leader. It is in just those situations when you are getting agitated because of the 'video' you have been watching that we want you to shout '*Stop! Think!*'. (Writing on a whiteboard)

1. What is my problem, exactly? E.g. 'I want to get home'.
2. What are the options?
    (a) wait another ten minutes
    (b) ring for a taxi
    (c) ring a friend
    (d) try walking home, etc.
3. Choose an option.
4. See how the option works out and if necessary go back to the 'menu' at (2).

This *Stop! Think!* problem-solving procedure means that you sort things out rather than let your mind go dancing.

Mary. It all sounds so simple sitting here but when it happens to you . . .

Co-leader. Some people find it helps to carry around a reminder with them because you can easily be caught off guard e.g., a piece of card in your purse that has '*Stop!*' on one side and '*Think!*' on the other. Doing this can help you ignore the false alarms in your nervous system.

John. I think it is these damn false alarms that stop me getting to sleep.

Co-leader. Override the alarms by putting a favourite music tape on a portable cassette player when you go to bed. As your mind races increase the volume of the tape and reduce the volume as you relax. If you are not asleep by the end of the tape calmly get up, do not get angry with the alarms – that makes it worse. If you keep your cool your body will not let you go without the sleep that you need. Just go back to bed when you feel tired.

The core task in these sessions has been to help the PTSD client label and understand their emotional state and to view this formulation as a statement about a particular past experience rather than one carrying any implications for current interactions and engagement with life.

At the ninth session, for homework clients are asked to 'complete their story' by writing about how they could realistically move forward and what pitfalls might befall them.

Session Ten. Review and Relapse Prevention

The final session begins with group members discussing their hypothesised endings to their story and the problems that they may encounter. The rationale for this is that if clients construct and become familiar with a viable and adaptive 'video' of their future then they are likely to be sufficiently motivated to make it happen. The 'future video' should ideally represent a continuity from pre-trauma experiences, so that the basic personality and identity is still intact. Nevertheless, some changes are inevitable, as is evident in the following exchange.

Sarah. I have written that I probably will not be working in the shop, in the long run, another branch was robbed during the week. But I can see myself getting involved when the new grandchild arrives, my daughter is only taking maternity leave, I am actually looking forward to that. I have started going out locally. I am determined to get myself right for when this baby arrives and it could well come on the anniversary of the robbery!
Co-leader. That is a great way of seeing that your assailant does not have the last word on what that week or month means to you.
Leader. I think that is one of the main messages that we have been trying to get over in the programme, your trauma is not fixed in a tablet of stone, you really can change how it figures in your mind.

Mary. But there are some things that you can't change. It's five years since the incident now and the legal side is still not sorted. Every time I get a solicitor's letter I go sick, the thought of appearing in Court kills me, all I want is an apology. I am not really interested in the money, I just want someone to say 'Sorry'. Court dates keep getting changed for stupid reasons. I don't know whether I am pleased or vexed.

Leader. Is the prospect of Court stopping you getting on with your life Mary?

Mary. Yes, with more letters of late I feel in limbo.

Leader. Sounds like you are expecting 'understanding' from the Court and legal process. But your opposition is not a person, it is an organization (the insurers of an hotel where Mary was caught in a fire) who will be battling against you; people in your position do not end up feeling 'understood'. The legal process simply puts into monetary terms your distress, it is always 'cold'.

Mary. I wonder why I bother!

Sarah. If you did not you would kick yourself.

Mary. That's probably true.

Co-leader. Maybe, Mary, if you can accept that understanding from the legal process is not on, you can alter the status of the proceedings in your mind, crossing the legal bridges when you come to them. It would be sad if you stopped yourself making the most of each day whilst you waited for a legal conclusion only to find that nobody actually says 'Sorry' anyway.

Mary. I had to see the psychiatrist for the insurers again last week, and he kept going on and on about my brother's death twelve months before the fire. I told him I was on tablets for a couple of months after Keith but he went on and on. I said he was upsetting me but he said that he was only doing what would be done in Court.

Leader. I am afraid Mary that they will probably try to argue that your distress is due largely to your brother's death and not the fire.

Mary. That's a disgrace!

Co-leader. You have to see it just as an attempt of the other side to avoid parting with money. It is nothing to do with you personally because they do not know you.

Mary. So what you're saying is that I am better seeing the whole legal thing as a side issue about money?

Co-leader. That's about it. Place it in the background of your life, not the foreground, deal with it when you have to, it will just be two or three probably unpleasant days in your life. Put the Court appearance into context the way you have the fire itself.

Mary. I think I might need to give you a ring at the time.
Co-leader. That's fine.

Each client will have their own possible relapse precipitants. Using the problem-solving procedure described in Sessions Seven to Nine, ways of coping with these should be elaborated. One option to be considered is further contact with the group leaders or with other group members. It is important to stress that it is unrealistic to expect that certain situations will not crop up which will knock them 'off balance' but that using the coping strategies taught in the course and with the support of fellow participants they will 'regain their balance', they will not be 'knocked over', much less 'knocked out'. The main message to be conveyed is that it is anticipated that they will be 'copers' in difficult times rather than 'masters', thus avoiding the tyranny of unrealistic expectations. Finally the programme is audited by re-administration of the psychological tests for PTSD symptomatology (PENN, IES) and co-morbid depression (BDI).

7

DEPRESSION

Clients with depression can account for as much as 50 per cent of a counsellor's workload. Depression has been termed the 'common cold' of mental health. Whilst this term reflects the ubiquity of the problem it belies its seriousness – about 15 per cent of depressed clients ultimately commit suicide. About 20 per cent of adult women and 10 per cent of men experience at least one major depressive episode. If a person has one episode of depression there is about a 50 per cent chance of a recurrence, and thereafter episodes are likely to recur about every four years.

This pattern of depression is consistent with a vulnerability model of the disorder, in which it is suggested that the depression-prone individual has trait-like qualities that will usher in the full-blown disorder if pertinent events take place. For example Beck (1987) identified two modes of personality amongst depressed clients, sociotropy and autonomy. Sociotropy is characterized by an excessive reliance on approval by others for a sense of self-worth, whilst the autonomous individual defines themselves almost entirely in terms of achievements. Thus a sociotrope would be free of depression so long as there is no major disruption of a relationship, whilst the autonomous individual would be free of depression so long as they were not prevented from achieving.

Vulnerability models can be conceptualized as a lock-and-key phenomenon. The lock to a person's depression might be being a sociotrope, the key that turns the lock and opens the door to depression might be the breakdown of their marriage – a matching key and lock are needed. A variety of other 'locks' for depression have been suggested, including dysfunctional attitudes (Beck 1987), attributional styles (Seligman 1981) and personality disorders (Beck et al. 1990).

Dysfunctional attitudes are the assumptions that commonly underlie the idiosyncratic thoughts typical of depression e.g. 'I am nothing if a person I love does not love me.' A collection of such dysfunctional attitudes is presented in the Dysfunctional Attitude Scale (Weissman and Beck 1979: reproduced in Scott 1989).

Seligman (1981) has suggested that depressed clients have a maladaptive attributional style so that negative events are attributed to internal, stable and global causes and positive events to external, unstable and specific causes. Thus a depressed person surprised that they have actually passed a particular exam might attribute this to a lenient teacher (an external cause), to being lucky this time (an unstable cause), and happening to be 'on song' on the day because they had just been invited to take a holiday trip (a specific cause). A depressed person failing the exam might tell themselves that they did not have the requisite brain power (an internal cause), that they had always been useless (a stable cause) and that they were inadequate in every department of their life (a global cause).

Clients with personality disorders appear to be particularly likely to possess dysfunctional attitudes and to have a maladaptive attributional style.

> Individuals with personality disorders show the same repetitive behaviours in many more situations than do other people. The typical maladaptive schemas in personality disorders are evoked across many or even most situations, have a compulsive quality, and are less easy to control or modify than are their counterparts in other people . . . In sum, relative to other people, their dysfunctional attitudes and behaviours are overgeneralized, inflexible, imperative and resistant to change (Beck *et al.* 1990, p. 29).

As about 50 per cent of depressed clients have a personality disorder this group presents a particular therapeutic challenge.

Champion and Power's (1995) model of depression involving the loss of an overvalued role is also in essence a vulnerability model, as the reasons why a role is overvalued probably have their roots in particular dysfunctional attitudes or personal styles. It takes an event (a key) to ensure the loss of the role. It is a pragmatic matter, to be determined by research across cases and by collaboration between counsellor and client in individual cases, whether depression is better tackled at the 'atomic' level of dysfunctional attitudes, etc. or at the larger, more 'molecular', level of roles, or by some judicious combination of both levels. The latter, combined, approach is adopted in this chapter.

INITIAL ASSESSMENT AND AUDIT

In the absence of any obvious co-existing disorder such as panic disorder or the experience of an extreme trauma, a score above 10 on the depression subscale of the Hospital Anxiety and Depression (HAD) Scale (Snaith and Zigmond, 1983) indicates a probable clinical case of depression. This should however be confirmed by asking open ended questions for each of the DSM IV (American Psychiatric Association 1994) diagnostic criteria for major depressive disorder (reproduced in Appendix A). Sample questions from the SCID interview (Structured Clinical Interview for DSM-III-R. Spitzer *et al.* 1990) are:

> Re criterion one – depressed mood most of the day nearly every day,
> 'In the last month . . . has there been a period of time when you were feeling depressed or down most of the day nearly every day?' ('What was that like?')
> IF YES. 'How long did it last?' ('As long as two weeks?');
> Re criterion two – markedly diminished interest or pleasure in all, or almost all, activities most of the day nearly every day
> 'What about being less interested in most things or unable to enjoy the things you used to enjoy?' ('What was that like?')
> IF YES. 'Was it nearly every day?', 'How long did it last?' ('As long as two weeks?').

The interview, rather than a scale score, should be given the greater weighting, the latter is simply a measure of severity and a pointer to the sort of questions that are likely to be pertinent. The questions in the interview are used to determine whether the DSM criteria are met – they are a means to an end. Thus if a client exhibits a behaviour that clearly contradicts his or her verbal response, the behaviour is taken as being more salient. In this connection it can be useful to also see the depressed client's partner, who may provide a more accurate report of their behaviour. Depressed clients may not admit that they are depressed because of the stigma attached to the label, perhaps seeing it as a sign of weakness, or because they are thereby avoiding getting depressed about being depressed. The HAD is a good screening device for depressed clients but is not very sensitive to small improvements in functioning. By contrast the Beck Depression Inventory (BDI. Beck *et al*. 1961) is a noisy screening device, yielding many false positives, but is an excellent measure of even small improvements. The HAD and the BDI should be re-administered at the end of the programme, and at follow-up.

CONVEYING THE METAPHOR

One of the models of depression suggested by Beck (1987) is that depression is an attempt to conserve energy and not squander it on fruitless activity, and that this might have been an adaptive response in some circumstances in our evolutionary history. Building on this, depression can be described as follows.

Leader. Depression is rather like blowing a fuse in the nervous system, everything goes dead, you feel a shell, nothing tastes the same. It means that you are on strike for better pay and conditions, you have a 'Temporarily closed for repair' notice on the outside. When you have done the repair job on yourself you will open up for business again, but not before. Part of the repair will mean giving yourself permission to meet your own needs. You are of course free not to meet your own needs but if you carry on business as usual the fuse will blow again. There is no point in fixing an appliance by simply replacing one blown fuse with another.

SPECIAL CONSIDERATIONS FOR DEALING WITH DEPRESSED CLIENTS WITH PERSONALITY DISORDERS

A variety of cognitive–behavioural approaches to the counselling of the personality-disordered client have been developed (Beck *et al*. 1990; Young, 1994), though they are not yet empirically evaluated. Nevertheless, there is a consensus that the guidelines of Flemming and Pretzer (1990) given in Figure 7.1 should be applied.

Probably the major shift in emphasis from traditional cognitive–behavioural counselling to that designed for the personality-disordered client is in the emphasis on the therapeutic relationship. The client's impact on the counsellor can provide useful data as to how the client may be affecting others. The group sessions may furnish

GUIDELINES FOR COUNSELLING CLIENTS WITH PERSONALITY
DISORDERS

1. Interventions are most effective when based on an individualized
   conceptualization of the client's problems.
2. It is important for the counsellor and client to work collaboratively
   towards clearly identified and shared goals.
3. It is important to focus more than usual attention on the counsellor–
   client interaction.
4. Consider interventions that do not require extensive self-disclosure.
5. Interventions which increase the client's sense of self-efficacy often
   reduce the intensity of the client's symptomatology and facilitate
   other interventions.
6. The counsellor should not rely primarily on verbal interventions.
7. The counsellor should try to identify and address the client's fears
   before implementing changes.
8. The counsellor should anticipate problems with compliance.
9. The counsellor should not assume that the client exists in a
   reasonable or functional environment.
10. The counsellor must attend to his or her emotional reactions during
    the course of therapy.
11. The counsellor should be realistic regarding the length of therapy,
    goals for therapy, and standards for self-evaluation.

Figure 7.1   Guidelines for Counselling Clients with Personality Disorders

further data on how the client connects with others, and provides a laboratory in which they can experiment with new ways of making contact.

Young (1994) has suggested that the mental schemas of a personality-disordered client fall under one or more of the following five headings.

1. *Disconnection and rejection.* Expectation that one's needs for security, safety, stability, nurturance, empathy, sharing of feelings, acceptance and respect will not be met in a predictable manner.
2. *Impaired autonomy and performance.* Expectations about oneself and the environment that interfere with one's perceived ability to separate, survive, function independently or perform successfully.

3. *Impaired limits*. Deficiency in internal limits, responsibility to oth-
    ers, or long-term goal orientation. Leads to difficulty respecting the
    rights of others, making commitments, or setting and meeting per-
    sonal goals.
4. *Other-directedness*. An excessive focus on the desires, feelings and
    responses of others at the expense of one's own needs, in order to
    gain love and approval, maintain one's sense of connection, or
    avoid retaliation.
5. *Overvigilance and inhibition*. Excessive emphasis on controlling
    one's spontaneous feelings, impulses and choices in order to avoid
    making mistakes or on meeting rigid, internalized rules and expec-
    tations about performance and ethical behaviour, often at the ex-
    pense of happiness, self-expression, relaxation, close relationships
    or health.

Each of these schemas is reflected in particular maladaptive ways of
interacting with other people. Thus a combined group and individual
programme probably provides better access to these schemas. It is not
suggested that such schemas can be replaced but rather that as the
client becomes more aware of their operation and impact, they operate
less rigidly and they develop compensatory schemas for connecting
with others. Part of the group leader's task is therefore to highlight the
expression of the schemas, and to help the client discover alternative
ways of interacting, perhaps by suggesting that they copy the more
adaptive behaviour of another group member.

COMPLEMENTING THE GROUP PROGRAMME WITH INDIVIDUAL SESSIONS

Depressed clients are usually more resistant to engaging in a therapy
group than anxious clients. Consequently they need a great deal of
reassurance that they will not be forced to disclose anything that they
do not wish to, whilst at the same time being made to feel that their
unique personal problems will be addressed. This latter goal is
achieved by building in three individual sessions at the beginning of
the group programme to ensure adequate engagement. These individual sessions can take a more historical focus and will be particularly
important to those with a personality disorder. The content of these
early individual sessions is described first before the main group programme, though in practice they run concurrently.

Individual Sessions for Group Members

The purpose of the individual sessions is to troubleshoot any problems occurring in relation to the group and to address any material, past or present, that the individual might be too hesitant to express in the group. In these sessions the intent is not to resolve major issues for the client such as childhood abuse or neglect or difficulties with their partner, but to create a conceptual framework in which those matters might be addressed in an anonymous way in the group. If historical material and the client's ability to make satisfactory contact with others is not put somewhere on the agenda for the programme then the needs of depressed clients with personality disorders will not be met, so these needs should be addressed in the individual sessions.

The first individual session begins by eliciting from the client how they felt attending the first group session and distilling any reservations they have about attending subsequent group sessions. The concern is to tackle anything that might prevent the client from integrating into the group. Thus the focus is not usually on the technical matter of the homework set at the end of the first group session. Clients typically report a mix of emotions: on the one hand saying it was good to know that other people who appeared ordinary had the same problems as themselves but nevertheless concerned that perhaps they didn't fit in, afraid that they said too much or too little. The leader can respond that this is in fact what most group members say, which can be amusingly summed up as each member of the group saying 'They are like me, but I am not like them.'

It is an important learning point for the likely one third of the group who will have an avoidant personality disorder to appreciate that everybody regards the others as ordinary. This can then be used as a springboard for suggesting that the 'audience of life' is mixed: there are others out there like group members as well as the minority who are critical and demeaning. However, the autonomous client can have problems being regarded as ordinary as their passport to acceptability rests on being seen to have achieved. Such clients might complain about the pace of the group or of someone in the group going off at a tangent. In such cases the group leader might underline a contribution the client made to the group or, better still, if possible, how their contribution positively affected another group member, indicating that they had connected and contributed.

There is an even greater need to stress examples of connectedness for those with the 'odd' personality disorders (paranoid, schizoid, schizotypal) who regard relationships as 'messy' and for the narcissistic personality disorder who typically lacks empathy. Clients with a borderline personality disorder often show abrupt mood changes within the group session, being very vocal at one point in the group and then becoming restless and hiding at a later point. These shifts of involvement should become a focus because they often mirror the borderline's interactions with others; approaching, getting close, fearing that their negative identity might be revealed, and abruptly retreating.

These sessions should also be used to trace the historical development of the client's depression – that is, to distil the client's narrative of where they have been – and to summarize it in such a way, if possible pictorially, that its effects on current life are rendered obvious. Having made the influence and bias of the past explicit, better ways of managing it may then be elaborated.

The leader and co-leader will already have some understanding of the development of the client's depression from the initial assessment and possibly the first group session. The therapeutic task is to reflect back to the client their understanding of the circumstances surrounding their early maladaptive interpretation of self (EMIS) and their early maladaptive expectations of others (EMEO). The EMIS and EMEO have been hypothesized to be at the root of the depression of personality-disordered individuals (Scott *et al.* 1995a).

One way of doing this is to reflect back the client's history in age bands of, say, 5 years, in terms of external problems (e.g. parents arguing) and subjective responses (e.g. feeling frightened), and to ask the client to correct any mistakes or omissions. In this way it is possible to focus on the period of transition to the client's negative view of themselves. Knowing the circumstances at the time of first negative appraisal and expressing them in concrete terms (e.g. 'It started when I was put on the train to go and stay with an Aunt'), makes it possible for the client to then access the thought processes involved (e.g. 'I am too much trouble'). Because the EMIS is portrayed as a 'chance' product of circumstances, reflecting naivety, it is at least in principle open to reappraisal. However, the earlier the development of the EMIS, the more it will resemble an ingrained prejudice. The goal of the programme is not to uproot the prejudice but rather, by acknowledging it, to become able to nip its expression in the bud and to develop a set of compensatory skills.

The approach taken in the individual sessions is illustrated here by the case of Malcolm, a senior fireman – a station commander – severely depressed and with a borderline personality disorder. He had been referred by his GP because he appeared not to have got over the break-up of his relationship with his girlfriend six months previously. Malcolm had thought of suicide but worry about the effects on his aged mother prevented him acting on the idea. He also felt a responsibility to his three children, all born to different mothers, none of whom he had ever had any affection towards. Malcolm functioned well at work, respected for his fairness but known to be irascible and to not suffer fools gladly.

Because Malcolm had initially been thought to be a suicide risk by the referring GP a prime concern in the individual sessions was to check whether there were was any current suicidal intent. The more an individual has made detailed suicide plans the more likely they are to attempt suicide. Malcolm denied having any such plans though he confessed that sometimes he felt as if he would not mind not waking up the next morning. The next step is to make explicit the reasons behind the changes from passive wishing to active planning. In Malcolm's case, after initial referral he became more conscious of the potential effects of suicide on his mother, then a week before the first group session his first grandchild was born and he recalled being moved to tears when he held him. The absence of strong positive reasons to live are most likely to be predictive of suicidal behaviour. However, there were some further risk factors in Malcolm's case. His borderline personality disorder meant that he did tend to be impulsive and he also very occasionally had a bout of heavy drinking. It was agreed that strategies for both of these would be addressed in the course of the group programme and not in the individual sessions. Had there been serious suicidal intent Malcolm would have been withdrawn from the group programme and offered a programme of individual sessions.

Malcolm reported a childhood in which his father had been cold, distant and authoritarian. His mother was warm but preoccupied with placating his father and looking after the four younger children. At age 12 he was buggered by an uncle of a friend. His parents were very annoyed when he subsequently urinated and defecated on the bathroom floor at home and he felt unable to tell them why. Malcolm reported that 'I felt ashamed, as though I had done something.' Some months later he saw his assailant on a bus when he was going to school and began playing truant. This led to further conflicts with his parents. He said that by the time he was 19 he had really begun to hate himself and tried to cut his penis off. Malcolm's promiscuous relationships with women became too numerous to count. However the relationship with his last girlfriend, Eva, had particularly devastated him because he had become absolutely sure that she really cared for him but the more he ruminated on this the more destructive his behaviour towards her became. Ultimately she left for her own safety but her parting words had stung him. 'How can anyone so very professional be privately so pathetic?' This history was collected over the initial assessment and the first individual session.

At the second individual session a linear diagram of Malcolm's story was drawn – Figure 7.2. Each significant event was elaborated with (a) his view of himself 'I am . . .', (b) his personal world 'Life is . . .' and (c) the consequent strategies used 'So, I . . .'.

The advantage of summarizing the client's story in the form of a chain is that the pivotal role of certain events becomes clearer. At any point in the chain it is possible to say that 'But for . . .' taking a particular view of self and personal world, certain strategies ('So I . . .') would not have been employed, i.e. the chain would have been broken. It is extremely important to remind clients of how naive they were at the times they first began their negative – and persistent – interpretations of themselves and their personal world.

In Malcolm's case he was asked about his 12-year-old nephew Simon, whom he described as 'dizzy'. Then Malcolm was asked how Simon would handle the sort of assault he had been subjected to. Instead of answering the question Malcolm went into a tirade detailing the vengeance he would exact upon such an assailant. This allowed the leader to point out that he was blaming the assailant, not Simon, to which Malcolm replied in a puzzled tone.

Malcolm. Well, of course.
Leader. But what if Simon said he felt 'dirty'?
Malcolm. I would tell him not to be bloody stupid and take him fishing.

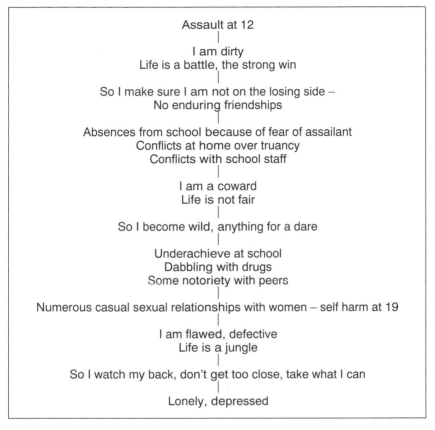

Figure 7.2   Malcolm's Difficulties

Leader. Looking at the chain, if someone had told you not to take the feelings of being dirty seriously, regard them as a 'mental cold', carry on business as usual and go fishing, you would not have felt so bad about yourself and you would not have regarded life as a battle. You might have felt that despite everything someone can really be there for you.

Malcolm. The stupid thing is that I don't really know how my parents would have reacted if I had told them.

Leader. Do you think Simon would tell his parents in those sort of circumstances?

Malcolm. I honestly don't know.

Leader. Would you blame him?

Malcolm. No, he's just a harmless daft kid, everyone wonders whether there is anything inside his head, the things he does.

Leader. It was those early events and ways of thinking about yourself and your world that started you rolling downhill, as it were. As you went down you gathered speed, and there were many nasty collisions with others, but how responsible for those have you really been? Doesn't responsibility lie largely with the person who sent you rolling?

Malcolm. Yes, but I have to get my act together. I can't put it all down to something that happened thirty years ago.

Leader. OK, if we are talking about a responsibility pie, how much do you think your assailant has been responsible for your difficulties?

Malcolm. About 60 per cent.

Leader. And what about your parents for not creating an atmosphere in which you were freer to express your feelings?

Malcolm. Maybe 25 per cent.

Leader. That only leaves a thin slice of the cake, 15 per cent, for you.

Malcolm. OK, so what do I do now?

Leader. I think a major goal for you is going to be working on this excessive self-blame, reminding yourself how slim your slice of the cake is. It is going to be hard though, you can see from the chain you have spent years developing this prejudice against yourself. For starters, when you are in self-blame mode you are going to need to start comforting the 12-year-old Malcolm as you would Simon.

Malcolm. What about my relationships?

Leader. I think you will not get as cross with positive messages from girlfriends if you first of all accept yourself.

Malcolm. It is not just that though. As soon as management ask me to do anything, be a pilot station, to run our own budget, go on a specialist course somewhere, I would do it all without even thinking about my girlfriend.

Leader. Why do you think that might be?

Malcolm. It sounds like I have always got to prove myself.

Leader. It sounds like you are compensating for this excessively negative view of yourself.

Malcolm. Oh, I am fine with the lads in a meeting, I am a station commander then. When I am by myself I am just me. That I can't stand.

This extract illustrates the importance when dealing with highly charged historical material of moving away from the subject matter (the focus on Simon in Malcolm's case) to somewhat reduce emotional arousal in order for new information to be adequately processed, and then moving back to the client. Again a metaphor, a 'responsibility pie-chart', is used to tackle a prime target in depression – excessive self-blame. In contrast to traditional cognitive–behavioural therapy, historical material is used to explain why it is that erroneous beliefs about the self and personal world are resistant to change. These difficulties are likened to the problems of getting through to someone who has 'a prejudice', again a metaphor. Finally there is a focus on behaviour that in a sense is quite the opposite of what one might expect from a depressed person's negative self-image – compensatory behaviour.

In the third individual session the client's handling of the historical material and the effects of any present compensatory behaviours are the focus. Malcolm was finding that sometimes, rather than comforting the young Malcolm, he was getting angry with him, wanting to shout at him. In fact he was finding that he wanted to treat him in much the same fashion as his own father had treated him, with coolness and disdain. It was agreed that when he pictured the young Malcolm in his emotions he imagined Simon next to him and that he had to respond to both of them in the same way. However, he was to regard this as a counsel of perfection – something to be gradually striven for with many setbacks. In work he was asked to stop and think before he boasted about his achievements or bragged of people he knew such as local councillors as this was compensatory behaviour, and it was something which he acknowledged had also been an irritant to his partner in his last relationship.

There is a high degree of overlap between depression and marital distress, with about 50 per cent of depressives having severe marital problems (O'Leary and Beach 1990). These authors have also produced data which suggest that when both partners are motivated to improve the relationship, couples therapy improves both the marriage and the depression, whereas cognitive therapy impacts on the depression alone. Nevertheless, in the first author's clinical experience, to have both partners motivated is the exception rather than the rule. Consequently in any group programme for depression the state of some clients' relationships with their partners is going to be an issue.

The extent to which their relationship with their partner is a problem, and how it is causally related to the depression – whether it is the latter causing the former or a reciprocal interaction – is best determined in the privacy of the individual sessions. If the client does acknowledge that there have been periods of happiness in their marriage, then the task of improving matters can be presented as a matter of regaining lost ground, but where there is no history of any positive interactions it is difficult to suggest any reason for optimism. In some instances simply getting partners to timetable in behaviours that they both used to enjoy but have fallen by the wayside, perhaps because of the depression of one partner or the demands of young children, can be an important first step to improving the relationship. This can then be followed by allocating a slot in the day in which they observe the communication guidelines of Figure 7.3.

In using the guidelines clients are advised to adopt a 'both win' approach to the relationship, rather than remain focused on particular battles with an 'I win, you lose' mentality. For some clients, their partner's continued refusal to change has become totally unacceptable

---

COMMUNICATION GUIDELINES

1. In stating a problem, always begin with something positive.
2. Be specific.
3. Express your feelings.
4. Admit to your role in the problem.
5. Be brief when defining problems.
6. Discuss only one problem at a time.
7. Summarize what your partner has said and check with them that you have correctly understood them before making your reply.
8. Don't jump to conclusions, avoid 'mind reading', talk only about what you can see.
9. Be neutral rather than negative.
10. Focus on solutions.
11. A solution may be either an agreed behaviour change in one partner spelt out in very specific terms, or an agreement that one partner will simply accept, without necessarily liking, a particular behaviour, with no recriminations.

Figure 7.3   Communication Guidelines

but they feel unable to leave the relationship. In those instances having a client complete a decision matrix of the advantages and disadvantages of continuing the relationship both short and long term can be helpful. Self-help books such as Norwood (1986) can be useful for those whose relationship to their partner is more akin to an addiction than a healthy relationship.

The individual sessions should above all convey the message that highly personal issues can be addressed safely and that there are pathways out of these difficulties, with further markers relevant to each client being provided anonymously through the course of the group programme.

FORMAT OF TEN SESSION GROUP PROGRAMME FOR DEPRESSION

The group programme begins with the leaders introducing themselves and inviting each group member to introduce themselves. The leaders then stress the importance of maintaining group confidentiality, and suggest that issues they might be hesitant to raise in the group can be raised in the individual sessions or at the refreshment break at the end of each session.

Session One. Acceptance of Depression and Activity Scheduling

The session begins with a restatement of the metaphor for depression discussed earlier and probably introduced first at the initial assessment.

Leader. Depression is a signal for change. It's as if you're driving and the fuel gauge shows empty, and provided you heed the signal and call into the garage for petrol everything is well. However, some people might just get cross with the fuel gauge, and carry on their business, then they will come to a total stop, with major problems. Depression should lead you to ask questions such as 'Why haven't I been making any space for my needs?', 'How can I begin meeting my needs?' What do people think about that?
Brian. It seems so self-indulgent.

Leader. But can you take anyone anywhere if you do not call in for petrol?

Brian. I suppose not, but up until recently I just did things without having to give them a second thought. I was always on the go.

This highlights one of the major problems for depressed clients – the loss of an active healthy role for no explicable reason, leading to a depression about depression.

Leader. Maybe it is as if you were driving your car constantly at 70 m.p.h., Brian. If it is built for cruising at 50 m.p.h., eventually it is not going to perform too well.

Brian. My wife keeps saying I should say 'No' to things, but that is just the way I have always been.

Leader. Just because you have always had the foot down on the accelerator pedal doesn't mean you always must.

From this extract one might hypothesize that the client is a sociotrope, and his excessive need for the approval of others might need to be tackled in the framework of the more explicitly cognitive aspects of the group programme covered in later sessions.

Diana. I have just come to a grinding halt since having the baby eighteen months ago. I don't do anything. I am not fair on my husband, just want him at home all the time. He ends up going to the shops for me. The health visitor said it is post-natal depression, but I don't think it is. I love the baby, he keeps me going.

Co-leader. Sounds like you are getting some sense of pleasure with the baby but are you getting any sense of achievement?

Here the co-leader is drawing attention to two important dimensions of Beck's cognitive therapy treatment for depression, that activities have to be balanced between those that give a sense of achievement and those that give a sense of pleasure.

Diana. I used to get a real buzz from my work, worked all sorts of hours and then the baby came [in tears]. But I do love him.

The client's depression is explicable in terms of Champion and Power's (1995) notion of an overvalued role.

Co-leader. It sounds, Diana, as if you have said to yourself that being at work is the only route to a sense of achievement and pleasure, and by implication it is not possible to create other routes.

Diana. I know, but it meant so much to me.

Co-leader. But it was only one way of getting a sense of achievement and pleasure.

Brian. But my depression makes me so useless, I am even getting my poor wife to answer the phone for me, she has to sort out the bills now. When I think of what I am putting her through (choking back the tears).

Leader. Does she complain, Brian?

Brian. No, she is very good.

Leader. So let me get this right, your wife is not complaining that you are not able to do tasks on the scale you could previously, is that right?

Brian. Yes, that's right.

Leader. I can't quite see why you or Diana need to blame yourself so. What advice would you give to Diana, Brian?

Brian. I suppose just do what you can, you will get there.

Leader. Wouldn't you say she should be blaming herself?

Brian. No, it's difficult being at home. I had to take early retirement from the Army and it takes some getting used to.

Co-leader. But this sounds like one law for mere humans who are allowed not to get depressed about being depressed, and another for your good self.

Brian. I take your point. You're saying I have to simply accept that I am depressed and go on from there.

Co-leader. Yes.

Malcolm. It would be easier if I could see it, if my arm was in plaster.

Diana. I know what you mean, sometimes I wonder am I making all this up?

Leader. Just because you can't see depression does not mean it is not real, you cannot see a virus but it is real. The starting point for tackling depression is Item 2 on the Handout [Figure 7.4] – accepting that you are not responsible for the problem of being depressed, only for working on a solution. Our task is to tackle one problem – depression – not two problems – depression and depression about depression.

Brian. You are right, my wife gets more upset about my constant apologizing for being depressed than she ever does over what she has to do as a consequence.

DEPRESSION HANDOUT ONE

Side One

MANAGING YOUR MOOD

1. BECOME ACTIVE

Plan into your week some activity that might lift your mood. It might be an activity that you used to enjoy or a completely new activity. Do not wait until you feel like doing these activities, if you are active eventually the taste for life comes back. Enjoyment is a bonus, to begin with praise yourself simply for having a go at the activity.

Note: It may be necessary to begin with to break down the task into small parts to get started, e.g. visit a friend for an hour instead of for a whole evening – this is better than not going at all!

2. DON'T APOLOGIZE FOR BEING DEPRESSED

Remind yourself that you are not responsible for the problem, only for working on its solution.

3. CHECK CAREFULLY TO SEE IF THERE IS A MORE REALISTIC WAY OF THINKING

When your mood dips do a 'slow motion action replay' of the particular situation, to get at what it sounds 'As if' you have said to yourself to make you feel the way you do – your automatic thoughts. Then ask yourself 'Do these automatic thoughts really make sense or are they an exaggeration?', 'Is there a more realistic way of thinking in this situation?' (Further useful questions are on Handout Two. You might be looking at the situation from an odd angle – ten mental viruses which can produce 'poor photography' are also listed on Handout Two.)

For example:

      Automatic thought –'Life is passing me by' (feeling down)

      Realistic thought – 'Life is passing everybody by, I'll feel better if I
        get stuck into something' (a bit better).

Try using the form on the reverse side.

Side Two

UNDERSTANDING YOUR 'LOWS' AND DIGGING YOUR WAY OUT

1. When did your mood dip? What, if anything, were you doing?

....

....

2. What did you feel?

....

....

Figure 7.4   Depression Handout One

3. What does it sound 'As if' you were saying to yourself at the time?

....

....

4. Had one of the ten 'viruses' (Handout Two) [see Figure 7.5] disturbed you? If yes, which one or ones?

....

....

5. What would have been a more realistic way of thinking and behaving?

....

....

6. What early maladaptive interpretation of yourself and/or expectations of others may have been involved?

....

....

Figure 7.4 *(continued)*

Malcolm. But what if you think you have played a big part in bringing on your depression in the first place?

[It is noted that, as we have seen, Malcolm has a burning issue regarding blaming himself for the past that is addressed in concurrent individual sessions, but within the group session the group leader talks in generalities.]

Leader. Usually if people examine closely the events leading up to the depression, at the time it was not reasonably foreseeable that they would lead in that direction. What we would like to look at more closely in the individual sessions is the chain of events leading up to each person's depression. For now we are encouraging you simply not to apologize for being depressed, but to focus on solutions. Item 1 on the Handout (Figure 7.4) is one of the important steps towards overcoming depression – activity scheduling.

Activity scheduling

One of the main functions of activity scheduling is to break the vicious circle of inertia which leads to guilt about inactivity, which leads to further passivity, and so on. The tendency towards inertia is part of the depressive's attempt to conserve energy. As discussed above it is crucial that clients do not apologize for the tendency because it at least means that they are doing a stock taking on traditional expenditures of energy and assessing what allocations of future energies would reap the best dividend. Consequently, relatively less energy is going to be available in the short term, but what there is has to be used to maximum effect. This constitutes a reframing of some of their inactivity in a more positive light. It is suggested to group members that the absence of potentially uplifting events timetabled into their week serves to maintain their depression. In some instances there has been a virtually lifelong absence of pleasant events and this is a major factor in the development of the client's depression. There are two dimensions of activities that are important, the first is the degree of pleasure that they evoke and the second is the extent of a sense of achievement. Some activities may load more on the pleasure dimension e.g. watching a football match, whilst others are more achievement oriented e.g. doing an academic course. The therapeutic goal is to ensure that clients develop a balance of activities that give both a sense of pleasure and a sense of achievement.

Though activity scheduling is an explicitly behavioural enterprise it implicitly challenges the cognitive style of most of the group members with personality disorders. It is commonly the case that depressed clients with obsessive–compulsive personality disorder have a history of preoccupation only with achievement-orientated activities. On the other hand depressed clients with dependent personality disorder have historically been unable to legitimate to themselves spending time on activities which give themselves pleasure. The depressed client with an avoidant personality disorder may well have under-achieved, fearing that if they attempted something and failed they would attract ridicule, adopting an attitude of 'better to not try than to fail'. Depressed clients with a narcissistic personality disorder may believe that no activity is required of them to make themselves happy, the responsibility for their happiness lying entirely with others, and that they are the victim of circumstance. Activity scheduling is introduced by inviting group members to read through Item 1 on the Handout (Figure 7.4) and asking for comments.

Stephanie. Just coming here each week is difficult enough, I can't get my friend Mary to baby-sit all the time.

Leader. What about your husband looking after them?

Stephanie. Hmm, he looks after them a bit on a Sunday afternoon when I go to visit my parents.

Leader. Is that a break for you?

Stephanie. Not really, my parents have so many problems, there is no getting through to them, and as for my sister who lives with them she is deranged, she should be here not me. I always come away feeling worse, get home, he moans at me for having a long face, has his tea and goes to the pub.

Co-leader. Sounds like you are Cinderella, overloaded trying to rescue everyone at your parents' home and then taking virtually total responsibility for everyone at home. Maybe one of the reasons you have got down is that there is no space for Stephanie as a person, she is stuck in roles. daughter, sister, wife and mother. Whatever happened to Stephanie? Is Cinderella going to have a ball?

Stephanie. (laughing) I could do with a Prince Charming rather than this slob at home!

The use of fables is a powerful way of opening up for consideration alternative endings to the client's life story, and is a particularly appropriate way of overcoming the inertia present in depression, sufficiently for the individual to begin constructing a new life. Because they are fables they are not seen by clients as a direct threat, their relevance can be distilled without the emotional over-arousal which would impede information processing.

Co-leader. What could you do for yourself this week, Stephanie?

Stephanie. I have threatened my husband that I will leave the children with his mother one night, but he will not let me.

Co-leader. Why?

Stephanie. Probably because his mother will tell him off for being out at the pub all the time just like his father.

Co-leader. Do you get on with your mother-in-law?

Stephanie. Oh yes, she is great, but she has had a hard life, so much to put up with. Father-in-law was an alcoholic, they separated, then got back together again just before he died. He had mellowed then, they got closest then of all times. Mother-in-law doesn't do anything now. I think she may be depressed.

Leader. Perhaps she might enjoy having the children for a couple of hours one night?

Stephanie. Yes she might, I could maybe go to line-dancing with Mary.

The co-leader had noted the impact of Stephanie's marriage on her, and that she was following in the footsteps of her mother-in-law, perhaps using the latter as a role model, but decided that these concerns were probably better addressed at this stage in the concurrent individual sessions, and opted to retain a prime focus on the activity scheduling.

Because the inertia of depressed clients is so pervasive, it is emphasized that it is important to schedule activities at specific times, as vague commitments such as 'I will go swimming in the week' tend not to be acted upon. Group members are asked to engage another person in the scheduled activity if at all possible, so that the fear of letting them down by not keeping to the appointment presses them into action. Most depressed clients' response to invitations to activity issued by friends or family members has been to say 'I will wait to see how I feel', with subsequent displays of inertia. It is necessary to ensure that a client's activity level is not determined by their emotional state. The first step towards achieving this is to point out that if their feelings are allowed to rule they will be inactive, with no chance of experiencing any uplifts, but if they are active they open up the possibility of being pleasantly surprised. There has to be an acceptance that, to begin with, probably most of the scheduled activities will leave them cold and that they should not expect enjoyment but simply praise themselves for being active at this stage (i.e. regard engagement as an achievement).

One of the strengths of activity scheduling is that it implies that the client can potentially influence their mood by what they do, lessening the sense of helplessness. To begin to convey the message that mood is controllable, group members can be invited to discuss low spots in their week. Typical low spots are first thing in the morning when clients cannot get started or perhaps late Sunday afternoon when there is little activity and people tend to be with significant others. Discussion then takes place on the different ways each member might handle their low spots. The client's current way of handling their low spots should be presented as but one choice from a menu of options, with no inevitability about their response. Some options on the menu may require much more energy than the client currently has available, and it is important that the client selects an option that they believe they have the capacity to discharge as well as opening up the possibility of making a difference.

For homework, clients are asked to complete a diary every morning, afternoon and evening of what they have done, and to rate each activity on a 0–10 scale, for the sense of Pleasure it brought (a P score) and for the sense of Achievement (an A score). This record can then provide data on the influence of activity level on mood and can help to counter the depressive's belief that they are always depressed.

Sessions Two to Four. Identifying and Challenging Automatic Thoughts and Thought Processes

The second session starts with a review of the homework set at the previous session, activity scheduling. The primary task in these sessions is to introduce clients to the idea that it is largely their negative interpretation of themselves and their personal world that fuels the depression rather than past history or current circumstance, and then to suggest that it is possible to view themselves and their world from a different and more realistic angle, thereby countering this negative view. To these ends clients are taught how to adopt the style of the TV detective Columbo in questioning both the negative content of their automatic thoughts and their ways of processing information.

As the group assembles the leaders collect the diaries of the week's activities, noting the 'lows' and the 'highs' on pleasure and achievement for each individual. In reviewing the activity schedules in the group the goal is to have the clients attribute elevations of mood to activity. Inevitably group members' experiences of activity scheduling will have been mixed. The right tone can be set by first focusing on a client whose diary clearly indicates some benefit from the strategy and then problem-solving with those who have been less successful, thereby preventing their negative experiences lowering the mood of the group.

Leader. Looks like your mood was fairly good when gardening yesterday Brian, you put a 5 for pleasure and a 6 for achievement.
Brian. Yes, I needed to clear the autumn leaves and plant some bulbs for next year before it is too late. I have been putting it off and off.
Leader. On a scale of 1 to 10, Brian, how did you feel before you went out into the garden yesterday?
Brian. Probably about 3.
Leader. So your actual experience was a little better than your expectation?

Brian. Yes, I think that is right.

Leader. One of the ways of motivating yourself is to remember that there is usually a gap between expectation and experience. Perhaps remembering the two numbers involved as in Brian's case can be a quick way of getting started.

Co-leader. Malcolm, your mood seems to have been slightly better on the mornings that you got up, had a shower and went to buy a morning paper.

Malcolm. True, but I was still pretty miserable.

Co-leader. At this stage it is often more a question of praising yourself for the activity rather than expecting a marked change in mood.

Stephanie. I don't think I can praise myself for going line-dancing, even though I enjoyed it when I was there. Afterwards I collected the children from my mother-in-law's, then my husband came in just as I was finishing putting the children to bed. He created a scene about the children going to bed too late, the children were frightened, I was too. We've not spoken since.

Morag. I could not cope with that.

Stephanie. It's a case of having to.

Malcolm. What, financially?

Stephanie. That and then there is the house, it is in both our names. The children love him. It is only that he is with them so little, that when he is he spoils them.

Co-leader. You seem to be getting drawn, Stephanie, like a magnet, along the same line as your mother-in-law.

Stephanie. I can see it is like a roller coaster. I have got to get off but I am terrified of even more damage.

Morag. It makes me think that I don't have any real problems!

Leader. I would have thought that having to handle someone like your mother, Morag, would be – how can I put it politely – a 'challenge' for anyone!

Morag. I get so used to her, that I don't think of her as a problem.

Leader. But looking at the activity schedule your mood went down to 2 after a telephone conversation with your mother.

Morag. Oh that, I was telling her about my cold and she interrupted me and told me that I didn't need to see a 'shrink' but that I would need one if I had all her problems. I was intending to start making patchwork quilts again but after that I could not be bothered. I looked at some pills I had and a bottle of champagne, then my husband rang, and I suddenly came out of it and began to think of the baby.

Leader. It is important to carry on with your activities, be they line-dancing or quilt making, even if you are knocked off balance by events. The activity constitutes a restoring force.

In each of the subsequent group sessions some time is allotted to reviewing members' activity levels. But the main focus in the second and third sessions is on teaching clients to stand back from their automatic thoughts and thought process in order to critically evaluate them. The leader can provide an introduction.

Leader. Have you ever noticed how much easier it is to solve friend's problems than your own? It is because with friend's problems you can stand back, you can see the wood for the trees. What we were planning to move on to today is teaching you how to stand back from your own mental processes. When you start to feel that your mental processes have become negative, we want you to use that as a signal to detach yourself, stand back and ask questions about your thought content, or what we call automatic thoughts. The style of questioning is that of the TV detective Columbo. Imagine you have found, say, that the milkman has not left any milk this morning and you are furious, threatening to cancel milk deliveries, and your partner is unruffled and replies to your protestations with 'I need to go down to the shops for a newspaper anyway, I'll collect some milk while I am there.' If you did a slow motion action replay of your reaction, you might find that it is as if you were thinking 'This is the end of the world, the milkman's let me down, everyone lets me down, it's not fair.' Using Question (3) on the 'Columbo vs Negative Automatic Thoughts' Handout (the first part of Figure 7.5) might lead you to think that your partner's way of viewing the situation might merit serious consideration. Then using Question (5) you might ask whether saying 'It's not fair' helps you achieve the goal of having a decent breakfast. Further asking yourself Question (6) might lead you to reflect that whenever things do not go exactly your way, you automatically assume deliberate intent on the part of the wrongdoer, this gets you emotionally distressed and interferes with accomplishing anything. Any comments?

Brian. Same bloody milkman as us! No, I see what you mean.

Co-leader. There is a summary of what we are asking you to do – Item (3) on side one of the first Handout (Figure 7.4) – and we would like to review how you get on with that over the next couple of sessions.

COLUMBO VERSUS NEGATIVE AUTOMATIC THOUGHTS

In the style of the TV detective Columbo ask yourself the following sorts of questions when you encounter a negative automatic thought.

1. How true is that automatic thought? Is there a grain of truth in it? Is it 50% true? Or maybe 75% true?
2. Is this thought consistent? If I would make allowances for a friend in a similar situation or with a similar history, then why not also for me?
3. Who else says that the way I am looking at the situation is the only way? Would someone else's way of looking at it be better?
4. Is this thought useful? Does it get me anywhere?
5. Does this thought move me closer to or further away from achieving my goal?
6. Is there another way of thinking that would help me better achieve my goal?
7. Would another goal be more appropriate?

Some people find it easier to write down their automatic thoughts ('What was I thinking?') at the time, and then try to write down more realistic and helpful thoughts.

Watch Out For the Following Mental Viruses

1. ALL-OR-NOTHING THINKING: You see things in black-and-white categories. If your performance falls short of perfect, you see yourself as a total failure.
2. OVERGENERALIZATION: You see a single negative event as proof of a never-ending pattern of defeat.
3. MENTAL FILTER: You pick out a single negative detail and dwell on it exclusively so that your vision of all reality becomes darkened, like the drop of ink that discolours the entire beaker of water.
4. DISQUALIFYING THE POSITIVE: You reject positive experiences by insisting 'they don't count' for some reason or another. In this way you can maintain a negative belief that is contradicted by your every-day experiences.
5. JUMPING TO CONCLUSIONS: You make a negative interpretation even though there are no definite facts that convincingly support your conclusion.
   (a) *Mind reading:* You arbitrarily conclude that someone is reacting negatively to you, and you don't bother to check this out.
   (b) *Fortune teller error:* You anticipate that things will turn out badly, and then feel convinced that your prediction is an already established fact.

Figure 7.5   Depression Handout Two

6. MAGNIFICATION (CATASTROPHIZING) OR MINIMIZATION: You exaggerate the importance of things (such as mistakes or someone else's achievement) or you inappropriately shrink things until they appear tiny (your own desirable qualities). This is the 'binocular trick', looking through one end at the positives and through the other at the negatives.

7. EMOTIONAL REASONING: You assume that your negative feelings necessarily reflect how things are, e.g. automatically assuming that because you feel guilty you must be guilty or, more generally, 'I feel it, therefore it must be true'.

8. MUSTS, SHOULDS, HAVES and OUGHTS: You turn everything into an emergency with the use of these words, instead of keeping them for when they are truly necessary.

9. LABELLING AND MISLABELLING: Instead of simply acknowledging that you made a particular mistake, you label the whole of you, e.g. 'I am a failure'. Those who do not see things your way are labelled idiots or worse.

10. PERSONALIZATION: You see yourself as the cause of some external negative event which in fact you were not primarily responsible for.

Figure 7.5   *(continued)*

In the third or fourth session, depending on the time available, the group are introduced to the maladaptive ways of processing information that have been elaborated by Burns (1989) and are adapted on the second part of Handout Two 'Watch Out For The Following Mental Viruses', as shown in Figure 7.5. These are very similar to the ten errors of information processing in PTSD listed in Figure 6.7, but these thought patterns tend to manifest themselves in slightly different ways in different disorders.

There are no watertight distinctions between the ten categories. It is less important exactly which maladaptive thought process the client thinks that they are using, than that they feel they have a handle on their own distress mechanisms. Typically, a client habitually uses two or three of the categories.

The group is split into two with the leader taking one group and the co-leader the other and members discuss examples of the ten thought processes from their own life. It is suggested that clients are asked to write pertinent examples of their own thought processes on their copy of the Handout, to serve not only as an exemplar of the category but to highlight their continuing vulnerability. This list of biases in information processing can be used as a shorthand way for clients to check out the origins of their distress.

At the end of these sessions, for homework clients are asked to monitor changes of mood and note the associated automatic thoughts and behaviours as set out on side two of Handout One (Figure 7.4). It is explained to clients that sometimes they may be unable either to identify how they are disturbing themselves or to 'dig' themselves out, but if they bring the incomplete record to the next group session it might be possible to detect what is going wrong and suggest remedial action. The rationale for the pro-forma is that the client becomes alerted to their habitual ways of distressing themselves, is enabled to stand back from their experience, and is then able to rehearse a more adaptive cognitive and behavioural response.

Session Five. Problem Solving

The session starts with a review of clients' attempts at cognitive restructuring using the Thought Records of Handout One side two (Figure 7.4) and then problem-solving is introduced. The manner in which incomplete Thought Records are tackled is illustrated in the following extract.

Morag. I had a great weekend doing nothing much away at a cottage in the Lake District. I felt free, but as I got nearer home this black cloud came over me.

Leader. What was going through your mind then?

Morag. That's the trouble, nothing was going through my mind, nothing had happened.

Leader. I think sometimes it can be very difficult to spell out what the thoughts are and then it is best to examine the changes of feeling very closely to make a best guess at what you were thinking. When you were in the Lake District, Morag, you were feeling free. Is that right?

Morag. Yes I could just be me, a person, no demands, I was not daughter or nurse.

Leader. But getting back home you were feeling not free, possibly imprisoned by the demands of your different roles?

Morag. Yes I suppose so. The day after returning I rang in work sick. I am a District Nurse with the elderly and most of them are terminally ill. I couldn't face it. I felt so guilty because it is extra work for the other nurses.

Brian. How do you face that every day? It was bad enough when my mother was dying, but every day!

Morag. You get used to it.

Co-leader. But do you get used to it, isn't it something you should really do for a limited time then move on? Rather like social workers working in child protection move on.

Malcolm. It is like in my job as a firefighter, people often get promoted out of the way of the horrors or they go off with various physical injuries. Maybe we should be saying this is a young man's game and it's for a fixed time.

Morag. Part of the problem is that the bosses do not really want to know, we now have to audit absolutely everything, on top of the actual work with patients.

Leader. Sounds like at least one of the thoughts that you were having as you drove home was 'This whole job is beyond me'.

Morag. I think that is probably true.

Leader [addressing the group]. Which of the ten thought processes might be involved in that statement?

Malcolm. It seems a very black-and-white statement, very sweeping, all or nothing thinking.

Morag. I suppose it is. I am not so bad when I am actually with the patients, I do my professional bit then. It is winding myself up before I ever get into work and then the pressure back at the Health Centre, trying to enter everything on a damn computer.

Stephanie. There is some emotional reasoning going on too, you feel guilty letting your friends down in work, but I know from looking after my kids there is only so much you can do. You are not guilty, you need a break.

Morag. I think I do need a break but it is more than that, that is the problem.

This exchange shows that as clients begin to identify how other clients are disturbing themselves and offer corrective ways of thinking they are simultaneously having to reappraise their own experiences. The group is providing a safe and supportive context for each member to rewrite their life script and redefine their life roles. Problem-solving is a particularly efficacious and clear way of helping clients decide on and choose new roles.

PROBLEM SOLVING STEPS

1. Define the problem in terms as specific and concrete as possible.

2. Write down as many possible solutions to the problem as possible,
   going for quantity of solutions rather than quality:
   (a)
   (b)
   (c)
   (d)
   (e)

3. Go through the advantages and disadvantages of each solution, both
   short term and long term.

4. Choose a solution or combination of solutions.

5. Plan the steps necessary to implement the chosen solution:
   (1)
   (2)
   (3)

6. Review the solution in the light of experience, if necessary recycling
   to Step 2. and trying another solution.

Figure 7.6   Problem-solving Steps

Group members are introduced to problem-solving using the pro-
forma of Figure 7.6. The leader then takes an example of a problem
from one of the group members to illustrate the approach.

Leader. The first step in solving a problem is to spell out exactly what
that problem is. Doing this is like going down the sides of an hour
glass until you get to the middle. If we take Morag's problem as an
example, at first it was all very wide and vague – she just felt awful
coming home. Then we narrowed it down a bit to the job being a
major problem. Then we narrowed it down a bit further by asking
'Is it all of the job?' and, if I understand it properly, Morag seems to
be saying that it is the bureaucracy of the job that is the problem,
that is, if you like, at the neck of the hour glass. Getting as far as the
neck of the hour glass is often the most difficult of all the stages of
problem-solving. Once you know what the problem is, finding the
solution is much easier. You cannot really solve a problem until you
can spell it out – it is like going in to see your doctor and simply
saying 'I am not well'. If, alternatively, you can say that your knee
hurts when you extend it, then various possible solutions almost

instantly present themselves. So that to solve a problem you must not have any 'fuzzies'. Returning to Morag and Step 2 of the problem-solving process, the hour glass begins to widen out as we come up with a variety of options – even daft ones which sometimes turn out to be the best in the end. So that for Morag we might write.

(a) stay off work until they medically retire you;
(b) arrange to go back to teaching;
(c) apply for a job in a hospice;
(d) return to work and see how it works out if you are less particular about being accurate on the audit;
(e) work on a bank of nurses and just do locums of your choice.

The Leader then invites comment on the menu of options and Morag replied that she would do a combination of (c) and (e) if it were financially viable.

Leader. So to do Step 5 of the problem solving procedure, Morag, you would presumably first check the minimum amount of money you need each week, then ring a local hospice to make an appointment and see them about how often they would need you and what the rate of pay would be. This would take you to Step 6 and if the hospice was not viable back to one of the other options, your (a) to (e), at Step 2.
Morag. It all sounds so simple, I wonder why I haven't gone through that before?
Co-leader. Well there is actually a stage even before Step 1. that is called *problem orientation*. This means that people do not actually lock on to a problem, instead they become preoccupied with telling themselves how awful the situation is, how terrible other people are, how much of a failure they are themselves.
Morag. I have been telling myself I should be managing in work, colleagues manage.
Co-leader. That 'should' is one of the ten faulty thought processes and has stopped you being problem-orientated, that is, it has stopped you from locking onto the problem. It is often that people have, as it were, the strength to turn a nut with a spanner but they cannot get the spanner on the nut in the first place.
Malcolm. That is what I do with my girlfriend. She says something quite innocently that could be sorted and I just take off. I was saying to her that you had said it might be a good idea for us to both have

another session with you. She said fine but she could not make it next week because of pressures in work. Instead of sorting it out I took off, screamed, told her that if I was important enough she would take the time. Then when I shout she clams up and I get really frustrated.

Co-leader. I think that we have to get you to use a set of traffic lights when you get angry, to stop and think, to lock onto the present problem.

Malcolm. I can sort out problems in work, no problem. I think I use the problem-solving steps without realizing it but in my personal life it goes crazy.

Co-leader. It is often the case that some material from the past is what prevents people being problem-orientated, from locking onto the problem.

Clients with personality disorders seem to have particular difficulties with problem orientation. For example, the impulsive client with borderline personality disorder will often not perceive discrete problems at all, operating instead with all or nothing thinking such as 'Life is either the way I want it to be or it is awful'. Managing the historical material that can sabotage problem-solving is addressed in the next sessions.

Sessions Six to Nine. A New Script – Operating without the Prejudices of the Past and Recognizing and Avoiding a Toxic Atmosphere

The focus in the previous group sessions has been very present centred, involving activity scheduling, cognitive restructuring and problem-solving. However, the viability of these strategies will depend on the person's ability to come to terms with the past. Attempts to simply negate the past because it was painful often result in being overtaken by behaviours that, in their better moments, the person knows are inappropriate. To their horror the person may find themselves acting and thinking in the same manner as somebody that they vowed not to be like. The therapeutic task here is to ensure that group members do not use cognitive avoidance about painful past material nor live in the past.

The justification for focusing on painful past historical material can only be that it is exerting a detrimental effect on the present. There has to be concrete evidence of current impairment stemming from particular past experiences to legitimate attention. Thus the knowledge that a client was, say, adopted or that their parents divorced would not necessarily entail a focus on these events. Even the fact that such events, when discussed, result in tears is not evidence *per se* that the event has not been dealt with. It is possible to discuss any past painful event at a primarily perceptual level where the person remembers the feelings at the time of the experience and recalls the sensory experiences. Subsequently, though, they may have operated at a primarily conceptual level, putting the experience in an overall benign life context. The focus in these sessions is to enable clients to be on guard against historical 'saboteurs' to cognitive restructuring and problem-solving and to protect themselves. The more personality disordered the client the more ferocious will be the saboteurs. In essence, clients are writing a new script about who they are and the reactions that they can expect from others.

Session Six begins with a review of clients' problem-solving efforts since the last session.

Morag. I don't know what to do. I went to the Hospice, they would be happy to have me on the bank, and the money is reasonable, but it can really vary week to week how much you are used. I also talked to a friend of a friend who works on the bank and she tells me that there had been a directive from the chief executive of the Hospice to use the bank as little as possible because of cost.

Leader. So that option is still a bit vague. Would it be possible to work out, say, the average hours worked by the friend of a friend over the past month? And also whether she is worried enough about the future there to be making other employment plans?

Morag. That would give me something concrete to work on, I could get back to her.

Leader. Yes, at the moment we are at Step (2), refining what the options mean.

Morag. I keep thinking I should be making a decision and sticking to it.

Leader. But looking at the problem-solving pro forma you cannot do Step (4) until you have done Step (2).

Morag. I just think I would go on for ever dithering whether to do this or that and doing nothing.

Leader. Well you can't know that you will get stuck at Step (3) because you haven't reached it yet.

Morag. But I am like that, aren't I Stephanie? I must have driven you mad in the week. You said you didn't mind whether we went to see

Muriel's Wedding or *Emma* at the cinema and I must have changed my mind about 50 times.

Stephanie. It's just nice to meet someone worse than me!

Morag. Thanks, Steph!

Co-leader. I think if you think that there is a perfect solution to anything and that you can know it in advance you can delay forever. Most of the time there is no perfect solution, there are simply good and less good solutions. Usually you are acting on limited information and all you can do is to make a best guess.

Morag. I think I just get frightened of what I choose going wrong.

Co-leader. But chosen solutions rarely go totally wrong or totally right, whatever direction you go will probably involve at least some slight detour. It is having the confidence that whatever you choose you will always be able to sort something out somehow.

Morag. But I haven't got the energy for any further sorting out!

Leader. When you have set yourself the task of discovering the perfect solution you have already exhausted yourself. It is like searching for the Holy Grail.

Morag. I think it comes from my job, I like everything to be just so.

Co-leader. Life is more a muddling along, doing a series of experiments, seeing what happens and learning from the mistakes.

Brian. But Stephanie was happy to go to either picture, I don't see what the problem was, Morag.

Morag. I suspect it goes way back.

Leader. Often when we are overreacting to something, we are mixing up stuff from the past with the present, and it shows up our early basic assumptions about ourselves and significant others.

The above extract underlines some of the key features of problem-solving:

(a) Problems and options have to be precisely defined.
(b) Hassles are almost inevitable whichever solution is chosen.
(c) The consequences of any chosen solution are rarely catastrophic.
(d) Problems are usually solved by chipping away at them rather than being resolved by a single perfect solution.

The ways in which clients disturb themselves can become apparent in very trivial situations and can reflect their early maladaptive interpretation of self (EMIS) and early maladaptive expectations of others (EMEO). These historical influences are the major foci of the next two sessions.

The EMIS and EMEO are introduced using the last item of the Thought Record on side two of Handout One (Figure 7.4).

Leader. What I would like to do now is to try and illustrate how experiences from the past, often from as far back as childhood, can shape our reactions. If we use Morag's indecisiveness about choosing which film to go to as an example, what we are trying to do is fill in the last section, Question (6) of side two of Handout One. To do this we ask [writing on a whiteboard]

1. How did I look at myself earlier in life? You might answer this in age bands of say 2–5, 6–10, 11–14, 15–20, etc. If your way of looking at yourself changed negatively at a certain point, note carefully what happened in that year or over that period of years. What we are concerned to discover is when and how you developed an early maladaptive interpretation of your self (EMIS). We'd like you to each spend 10 minutes just writing down events that were pertinent to the development of a negative view of yourself.

2. What expectations of others have developed as a consequence of the earlier experiences? Here we are concerned to discover when and how you developed early maladaptive expectations of others (EMEO).
   Again please spend ten minutes just writing down events that were pertinent to the development of negative expectations of others.

Leader. How did you get on, Morag?

Morag. Well I can never remember ever feeling good about myself, there are no specific events, just that whatever I did for my mother was never good enough. I just felt inadequate, I thought that if I just tried harder it would all be OK but it never was. I would always come in the first four at school but my mother would just say 'Why didn't you come first?'

Leader. So the EMIS you developed was that you are flawed, not quite up to the mark, and the EMEO is that others are not going to accept you?

Morag. That's about it.

Leader. So the way this EMIS and EMEO has affected you is to make you very hesitant and anxious in relationships, and it shows in simple everyday matters like going to the cinema with Stephanie?

Morag. Sort of. I guess I knew as a child that not everyone was like my mother. I liked my Dad and I tried to get close, but my mother would create such a fuss and he was just so quiet and peaceful. Looking back I think that he was probably depressed, just took to his bed. Mother was and is just so powerful.

Leader. The next step is to recognize how much of your current distress has to do with current events and how much is to do with the influence of your EMIS and EMEO, i.e. we have to separate the distress that is of then and that which is of now. One way of tackling this is to join your hands together when you suspect your reactions are over the top, with the left-hand symbolizing *then* and the right hand symbolizing *now* and to abruptly separate them. After separating them you tell yourself that '*from now on* a more realistic interpretation of myself is . . . and a more realistic expectation of others is . . .'. In Morag's case this would first involve her mentally telling her mother that she was wrong to heap totally unrealistic expectations on her as a child, then going on to focus on the data that other people, like Stephanie, do like her, the audience in her life is not totally composed of people like her mother, it is a very varied audience. The EMIS and EMEO tend to act as a prejudice that wells up inside. You can't stop it welling up, if you try you will become more frustrated, but what you can do is to note its rise and step around it as soon as you can. With practice you get better able to spot it and step around it.

The saboteurs from the past can operate at different levels, at a micro level involving the EMIS and EMEO but also at a macro level involving outmoded roles. The problems caused by early fixed roles are addressed in the eighth and ninth sessions. Depressed clients, particularly those with a personality disorder, often have certain roles foisted on them in childhood. Attempts to move out of role are resisted by the rest of the 'cast'. Strategies used can involve flagrant guilt induction or, more subtly, expression of a concern not to rock the boat.

A common 'drama' is that the client was long ago auditioned for and bestowed the role of 'rescuer' by a parent who chose to play 'victim'. Eventually the 'rescuer' becomes exhausted, makes an aggressive complaint of unfairness, the apparent 'aggressiveness' is seized upon by the 'victim' and portrayed as evidence of being 'uncaring'. Unfortunately the 'rescuer' has never been given the opportunity to look at such allegations in a detached and critical manner, and they now see themselves as a 'persecutor'. Guilt ridden, they resolve ever more firmly to keep to the 'rescuer' role allowing the 'victim' and the drama to carry on. In some instances those playing roles in the client's drama have 'dramatic' or 'odd' personality disorders. The client has to be made aware of this, so as to not personalize the difficulties of interacting with them, and to enable them to develop realistic expectations and take steps to protect themselves from undue influence.

The material is introduced by discussing what roles group members felt they played in their family of origin and what roles they currently play.

Morag. I am definitely a 'rescuer' and mother's a 'victim'. On Saturday night she gave me a prescription that she wanted taking to the chemist. I said I would get it on Monday when the local shop opens but, oh no, mother wanted it on Sunday even though she had sufficient medication in. This meant I had to travel all the way into the city centre for a chemist on a Sunday.

Co-leader. Why did you 'have to'?

Morag. Because I wasn't doing anything special on Sunday and she would just moan to my sister Carol about me.

Co-leader. What would Carol say to you?

Morag. 'Oh it keeps her happy. She is getting old'.

Co-leader. So your sister would not blame you directly?

Morag. Oh no, she just makes me feel guilty and does not do anything herself. To make matters worse my mother thinks the sun shines out of her backside.

Co-leader. It suits your sister also to keep you as 'the rescuer'?

Morag. Yes, when my mother was in hospital it was me who was dispatched by Carol to find out from the nurse exactly what was going on. Looking back I felt I was about nine again being told what to do.

Leader. I think it is often useful, if you have a strong emotional reaction to something, to ask yourself when do you remember first experiencing these emotions, and it is probable that a similar drama to then is being enacted.

Malcolm. But it is doing something about it that is the difficulty.

Leader. You're right. You will, to begin with, find yourself in the allotted role, then it is a question of telling yourself that 'I have not chosen to audition for this role, a better role would be . . .'. In deciding on a new role there may be someone you know that you could copy or alternatively you may have to construct a new role.

Morag. In the family there is no one to copy, they are all into overreacting or so suppressed it's not true.

Malcolm. I developed a habit years ago in work if people were demanding the impossible of just ignoring what they said, or of giving just a one-line reply such as 'I will do it when I can'. I wouldn't explain myself – they give up on you in the end.

Co-leader. That is an excellent example of the broken-record technique. Like a needle stuck in the groove of a record you just repeat the same thing over and over, then you can't be got at. If you say anything more you give the others ammunition to use against you.

Morag. I suppose I should be like Malcolm with my mother but I just wish I could get through to her.

Leader. It sounds as if your mother has clearly shown that she has an inability to put herself in other people's shoes, and that she has to be the centre of attention. That sounds like she possibly has a narcissistic personality disorder. This means that she is essentially toxic and you will get gassed if you get too close for too long. If those close to you do have a dramatic personality disorder like Morag's mum you have to accept that they will not change and keep your distance.

Morag. If it was just my mother it would not be so bad but it's my sister as well. She never shows any interest in me or anyone. It is all what she wants to achieve. At the hospital as soon as I had found out what was wrong from the nurse, she left. No 'How are you, what are you doing now?'

Co-leader. As well as the dramatic personality disorders there are the 'odd' personality disorders, such as schizotypal personality disorder who see relationships as unnecessary and messy, and trying to connect with them is, I am afraid, doomed. I am afraid, Morag, it is probably a question of simply accepting how Carol is and looking to other sources of satisfaction in life.

Morag. But to get two personality disordered relatives in one family isn't fair!

Leader. No, but it doesn't mean you can't reach an at least just reasonably content watermark in your life as a whole.

Malcolm. It seems to amount to not flogging dead horses.

Brian. But you can't just abandon them!

Co-leader. I don't think we are suggesting abandoning. Just judicious contact, with realistic expectations.

The overall focus of Sessions Six to Nine is to help clients acknowledge their past, note the historical tendencies, and develop coping strategies to step around early maladaptive views of their self and their personal world.

Session Ten and Follow-up. Regaining Your Balance and Charting a Direction

In this final session the main focus for most of the group will be on relapse prevention. First, however, a brief overview of all the material covered in the sessions is conducted using the handouts. There are two reasons for this. First it reminds group members that they have learnt specific strategies in the course of the programme and implicitly suggests that any improvement in well being is in large part to do with the technical learning that they have successfully undertaken, and second it is a reminder of a reference point at times of future difficulties. This then paves the way for an explicit focus on relapse prevention. Inevitably one or two clients in a group will not yet have responded and for these the material covered is depicted as laying the foundation for recovery with the superstructure to be added in further individual sessions.

At this session group members are often quite anxious about whether they will be able to cope without the regular group sessions. This can be dealt with by stressing that their well-being is dependent on their use of what they have learnt in the sessions, both technically in terms of coping strategies and experientially in terms of the feedback others have given them about themselves and what the group might portray about the 'audience in life' in general. However it is viable to run separate anxiety and depression groups over the same time period then mix the groups for follow-up sessions arranged at six weeks, three months, six months and twelve months post-treatment. This lessens anxiety about the ending of the initial group.

In the follow-up sessions difficulties clients are having are addressed by underlining the relevance of some particular material already taught. But these follow-up sessions are as much about clients providing support for each other and the formation of friendships, thereby acting as further stepping stones to more rewarding interactions in their personal world. The initial follow-up session, if it is a combined group, is inevitably quite large, but rarely do all those who attended the specific programmes take advantage of a follow-up. These sessions are scheduled with a reducing frequency over a period of a year, allowing a 'weaning off' but nevertheless offering the opportunity for the formation of relationships. In some instances after the follow-up year group members have decided to periodically meet socially without the presence of the leaders, in a non-clinical environment.

In session ten, group members are asked to spend about thirty minutes in the session constructing 'first aid' notes. These should contain a list of the situations and thoughts that they have found typically 'start them rolling downhill' emotionally. Each of these scenarios should be written on a separate card and on the reverse of each card the client is asked to describe how they would apply a 'brake', i.e. what, specifically, they should do and what their self-talk should be. It is important that the first aid notes indicate that some slippage of mood is inevitable but with practice of the various strategies it can be stopped from gathering momentum. The essential message to be conveyed is that they now have the wherewithal to cope with their vulnerability to depression, but they should not regard themselves as cured. For this reason clients are asked to keep their first aid notes and session hand-outs accessible.

8

GROUP THERAPY, THERAPISTS AND FURTHER APPLICATIONS

The thought of running a group evokes initial apprehension in most counsellors. Typically the counsellor plays a 'horror video' of themselves drying up in front of an assembled multitude, or perhaps overwhelmed by a group's weight of human misery. There can be no doubt that running a group is typically more demanding than individual work, involving more monitoring, mental agility and, often, emotional labour, but the difficulties can easily be exaggerated. Certainly a minimum requirement is that the counsellor ought to already feel comfortable with individual counselling for the particular client disorder. Perhaps the greatest reason why group counselling is the exception rather than the rule is that heretofore there has been no obvious pay-off for the counsellor. However, with the greater insistence on audit and the constraints surrounding third party reimbursement in recent years, counsellors may be forced to re-evaluate their response to a group approach, at least to consider it as a component of an intervention plan. The personal gains for the counsellor in conducting a group intervention are unfortunately not that obvious in advance, but afterwards many group therapists report that it has added a variety to their work and that there is an exhilaration that comes from an underlining of their combined enabler, facilitator and teacher role. This leads on to the question of how counsellors can best prepare themselves for a group modality.

Ideally a group leader should have had prior opportunity to act as co-leader to a number of groups. Unfortunately this is not always practically possible. This should not deter the would-be group leader, though it will probably take them longer to develop a sense of competence. One very useful way of training counsellors for group leadership roles is to use a simulated group. One member of a counselling class elects to take the role of the group leader and four other counsellors take the role of the last person they have seen for the particular condition under examination in the group, whilst the rest of the class take the role of observers. The first group session in any of the programmes can be somewhat atypical compared to subsequent sessions and so it is most useful to simulate, say, the second session, in which the leader seeks to elicit feedback on the first homework exercise and then goes on to introduce some new material. Thus, for example, in a depression simulation the 'leader' would be asking members how they had fared with activity scheduling, drawing attention to any cognitive saboteurs of activity, then teaching cognitive disputation. The simulation is best run for about 30 minutes, followed by a further thirty minutes plenary discussion of the interaction. The Therapist Competency Checklist (Young and Beck 1980; reproduced in Scott *et al*. 1995a) can be used to ensure that the class keep their feedback and discussion on target but this instrument was designed with individual counselling in mind, and feedback should also be given about whether similarities between group members' experiences were underlined and whether some 'clients' were allowed to either dominate the group or fade into the background.

There are few disorders for which a group programme could not be a component of an intervention. Counsellors working in primary care may, however, meet so few clients with say, bulimia or obsessive–compulsive disorder that they are unlikely to be able to form a group. However with the increasing employment of counsellors in hospital departments or large-scale employee assistance programmes, groups for such disorders become more viable. Group programmes for bulimia (as described by Olmsted *et al*. 1991) and obsessive–compulsive disorder (as described by Enright, 1991) are therefore briefly outlined.

Olmsted *et al*. (1991) conducted a group educational programme for clients with Bulimia. This consisted of five 90 minute sessions over a 4 week period. Two sessions took place in the first week with weekly sessions for the subsequent 3 weeks. In the first session evidence that the human body has a drive to maintain a physiologically determined weight level was presented. Bingeing was framed as an attempt to restore homeostasis in an organism which is being underfed. Since bingeing occurs in the context of dieting, participants were encouraged to normalize their daily intake as a first step in overcoming bulimia. In the second session the pernicious effects of dieting, bingeing, and vomiting by laxative and diuretic abuse were outlined. Immediate cessation of purging behaviour was recommended because of the physical hazards involved and as a way of eliminating the negative reinforcement which vomiting provides for binge eating. The last three sessions focused on the sociocultural pressures on women to be thin, the process of evaluating oneself largely in terms of weight or appearance, myths about food and the effects of certain foods on weight, cognitive distortions surrounding eating and weight, and coping strategies for the period in which the group participants were attempting to normalize eating, but still had urges to binge. Olmsted *et al.* (1991) suggested that only patients who had not improved sufficiently with this group programme be subsequently offered individual cognitive–behaviour therapy, and that this might make for better use of scarce resources.

Enright (1991) conducted a group programme for obsessive–compulsive disorder (OCD) involving nine sessions held weekly. The first two sessions are used to give clients information on the prevalence of the condition and the theories suggested for its origin. Then the focus shifts to exploration of the situations in which the participants become obsessive, e.g. repeated hand washing after touching something, and the delineation of a preventive response, e.g. playing a hand-held computer game. For obsessive thoughts patients were asked to make a tape of their most disturbing repetitive thought and to listen to the tape daily, only switching off when not unduly distressed. Succeeding sessions focused on the relationship between mood and increased obsessional behaviour and the teaching of mood management strategies similar to those described in Chapter 7 here (e.g. Figure 7.4). As with the Olmsted *et al.* bulimia programme, Enright (1991) envisaged that the group programme would be supplemented by individual cognitive–behavioural therapy for those who did not improve sufficiently. Further cognitive conceptualizations and strategies for OCD that may be integrated into such a group programme have been described elsewhere (Scott *et al.* 1995a, pp. 86–89).

APPENDIX A. DSM IV DIAGNOSTIC CRITERIA FOR GENERALIZED ANXIETY DISORDER, PANIC DISORDER WITH AGORAPHOBIA, POSTTRAUMATIC STRESS DISORDER, AND DEPRESSION (American Psychiatric Association, 1994)

GENERALIZED ANXIETY DISORDER

A. Excessive anxiety and worry (apprehensive expectation), occurring more days than not for at least 6 months, about a number of events or activities (such as work or school performance).

B. The person finds it difficult to control the worry.

C. The anxiety and worry are associated with three (or more) of the following six symptoms (with at least some symptoms present for more days than not for the past 6 months). *Note:* Only one item is required in children.

1. restlessness or feeling keyed up or on edge
2. being easily fatigued
3. difficulty concentrating or mind going blank
4. irritability
5. muscle tension
6. sleep disturbance (difficulty falling or staying asleep, or restless unsatisfying sleep)

D.   The focus of the anxiety and worry is not confined to features of an Axis I disorder, e.g. the anxiety or worry is not about having a panic attack (as in panic disorder), being embarrassed in public (as in social phobia), being contaminated (as in obsessive–compulsive disorder), being away from home or close relatives (as in separation anxiety disorder), gaining weight (as in anorexia nervosa), having multiple physical complaints (as in somatization disorder), or having a serious illness (as in hypochondriasis), and the anxiety and worry do not occur exclusively during posttraumatic stress disorder.

E.   The anxiety, worry, or physical symptoms cause clinically significant distress or impairment in social, occupational, or other important areas of functioning.

F.   The disturbance is not due to the direct physiological effects of a substance (e.g. a drug of abuse, a medication) or a general medical condition (e.g. hyperthyroidism) and does not occur exclusively during a mood disorder, a psychotic disorder, or a pervasive developmental disorder.

PANIC DISORDER WITH AGORAPHOBIA

A.   Both (1) and (2):

1. recurrent unexpected panic attacks

    Panic Attack
    A discrete period of intense fear or discomfort, in which four (or more) of the following symptoms developed abruptly and reached a peak within 10 minutes:

    1. palpitations, pounding heart, or accelerated heart rate;
    2. sweating;

3.   trembling or shaking;
4.   sensations of shortness of breath or smothering;
5.   feeling of choking;
6.   chest pain or discomfort;
7.   nausea or abdominal distress;
8.   feeling dizzy, unsteady, lightheaded or faint;
9.   derealization (feelings of unreality) or depersonalization (being detached from oneself);
10. fear of losing control or going crazy;
11. fear of dying;
12. parathesias (numbness or tingling sensations);
13. chills or hot flushes.

2. at least one of the attacks has been followed by 1 month (or more) of one (or more) of the following:
    (a)   persistent concern about having additional attacks;
    (b)   worry about the implications of the attack or its consequences (e.g., losing control, having a heart attack, 'going crazy')
    (c)   a significant change in behaviour related to the attacks.

B. The presence of Agoraphobia
    Agoraphobia
    1.   Anxiety about being in places or situations from which escape might be difficult (or embarrassing) or in which help may not be available in the event of having an unexpected or situationally predisposed panic attack or panic-like symptoms. Agoraphobic fears typically involve characteristic clusters of situations that include being outside the home alone; being in a crowd or standing in a line; being on a bridge; and travelling in a bus, train, or automobile.
    Note. Consider the diagnosis of specific phobia if the avoidance is limited to one or only a few social situations, or social phobia if the avoidance is limited to social situations.
    2.   The situations are avoided (e.g. travel is restricted) or else are endured with marked distress or with anxiety about having a panic attack or panic-like symptoms, or require the presence of a companion.
    3.   The anxiety or phobic avoidance is not better accounted for by another mental disorder, such as social phobia (e.g., avoidance limited to social situations because of fear of embarrassment), specific phobia (e.g., avoidance limited to a single situation like

elevators), obsessive–compulsive disorder (e.g. avoidance of dirt in someone with an obsession about contamination), post-traumatic stress disorder (e.g. avoidance of stimuli associated with a severe stressor), or separation anxiety disorder (e.g. avoidance of leaving home or relatives).

C.   The panic attacks are not due to the direct physiological effects of a substance (e.g. a drug of abuse, a medication) or a general medical condition (e.g. hyperthyroidism).

D.   The panic attacks are not better accounted for by another mental disorder, such as social phobia (e.g. occurring on exposure to feared social situations), specific phobia (e.g. on exposure to a specific phobic situation), obsessive–compulsive disorder (e.g. on exposure to dirt in someone with an obsession about contamination), posttraumatic stress disorder (e.g. in response to stimuli associated with a severe stressor), or separation anxiety disorder (e.g. in response to being away from home or close relatives).

POSTTRAUMATIC STRESS DISORDER

A.   The person has been exposed to a traumatic event in which both of the following were present:

1.   the person experienced, witnessed, or was confronted with an event or events that involved actual or threatened death or serious injury, or a threat to the physical integrity of self or others.
2.   the person's response involved intense fear, helplessness, or horror. *Note.* In children, this may be expressed instead by disorganized or agitated behaviour.

B.   The traumatic event is persistently reexperienced in one (or more) of the following ways:

1.   recurrent and intrusive distressing recollections of the event, including images, thoughts, or perceptions. *Note.* In young children, repetitive play may occur in which themes or aspects of the trauma are expressed.
2.   recurrent distressing dreams of the event. *Note.* In children, there may be frightening dreams without recognizable content.

3. acting or feeling as if the traumatic event were recurring (includes a sense of reliving the experience, illusions, hallucinations, and dissociative flashback episodes, including those that occur on awakening or when intoxicated). *Note.* In young children, trauma-specific re-enactment may occur.
4. intense psychological distress at exposure to internal or external cues that symbolize or resemble an aspect of the traumatic event.
5. physiological reactivity on exposure to internal or external cues that symbolize or resemble an aspect of the traumatic event.

C. Persistent avoidance of stimuli associated with the trauma and numbing of general responsiveness (not present before the trauma), as indicated by three (or more) of the following:

1. efforts to avoid thoughts, feelings, or conversations associated with the trauma;
2. efforts to avoid activities, places, or people that arouse recollections of the trauma;
3. inability to recall an important aspect of the trauma;
4. markedly diminished interest or participation in significant activities;
5. feeling of detachment or estrangement from others;
6. restricted range of affect (e.g. unable to have loving feelings);
7. sense of a foreshortened future (e.g. does not expect to have a career, marriage, children, or a normal life span).

D. Persistent symptoms of increased arousal (not present before the trauma), as indicated by two (or more) of the following:

1. difficulty falling or staying asleep;
2. irritability or outbursts of anger;
3. difficulty concentrating;
4. hypervigilance;
5. exaggerated startle response.

E. Duration of the disturbance (symptoms in Criteria B, C, and D) is more than 1 month.

F. The disturbance causes clinically significant distress or impairment in social, occupational, or other important areas of functioning.

DEPRESSION

A.   Five (or more) of the following symptoms have been present during the same 2-week period and represent a change from previous
functioning; at least one of the symptoms is either (1) depressed mood
or (2) loss of interest or pleasure.

Note: Do not include symptoms that are clearly due to a general medical condition, or mood-incongruent delusions or hallucinations.

1.   Depressed mood most of the day, nearly every day, as indicated by
     either subjective reports (e.g. feels sad or empty) or observation
     made by others (e.g. appears tearful). *Note.* In children and adoles-
     cents can be irritable mood.
2.   Markedly diminished interest or pleasure in all, or almost all, ac-
     tivities most of the day, nearly every day (as indicated by either
     subjective account or observation made by others).
3.   Significant weight loss when not dieting or weight gain (e.g. a
     change of more than 5 per cent of body weight in a month), or
     decrease or increase in appetite nearly every day. *Note.* In children,
     consider failure to make expected weight gains.
4.   Insomnia or hypersomnia nearly every day.
5.   Psychomotor agitation or retardation nearly every day (observable
     by others, not merely subjective feelings of restlessness or being
     slowed down).
6.   Fatigue or loss of energy nearly every day.
7.   Feelings of worthlessness or excessive or inappropriate guilt
     (which may be delusional) nearly every day (not merely self-
     reproach or guilt about being sick).
8.   Diminished ability to think or concentrate, or indecisiveness,
     nearly every day (either by subjective account or as observed by
     others).
9.   Recurrent thoughts of death (not just fear of dying), recurrent sui-
     cidal ideation without a specific plan, or a suicide attempt or a
     specific plan for committing suicide.

B.   The symptoms do not meet criteria for a mixed episode (see DSM
IV, p. 165).

C.   The symptoms cause clinically significant distress or impairment
in social, occupational, or other important areas of functioning.

D.   The symptoms are not due to the direct physiological effects of a substance (e.g. a drug of abuse, a medication) or a general medical condition (e.g. hypothyroidism).

E.   The symptoms are not better accounted for by bereavement, i.e. after the loss of a loved one, the symptoms persist for longer than 2 months or are characterized by marked functional impairment, morbid preoccupation with worthlessness, suicidal ideation, psychotic symptoms, or psychomotor retardation.

APPENDIX B. DSM IV SUMMARY DESCRIPTIONS OF THE PERSONALITY DISORDERS AND EXAMPLES OF COGNITIVE CONTENT (American Psychiatric Association, 1994)

CLUSTER A – 'ODD'

1.   *Paranoid personality disorder* is a pattern of distrust and suspiciousness such that others' motives are interpreted as malevolent.

- 'Often people deliberately want to annoy me.'
- 'I cannot trust other people.'
- 'It isn't safe to confide in other people.'

2.   *Schizoid Personality Disorder* is a pattern of detachment from social relationships and a restricted range of emotional expression.

- 'Relationships are messy and interfere with freedom.'
- 'Intimate relations with other people are not important to me.'
- 'I shouldn't confide in others'.

3. *Schizotypal personality disorder* is a pattern of acute discomfort in close relationships, cognitive or perceptual distortions, and eccentricities of behaviour.

Cognitive content is much the same as schizoid above.

CLUSTER B – 'DRAMATIC'

4. *Antisocial personality disorder* is a pattern of disregard for, and violation of, the rights of others.

- 'Other people are weak and deserve to be taken.'
- 'If I want something I should do whatever is necessary to get it.'
- 'People will get at me if I don't get at them first.'

5. *Borderline personality disorder* is a pattern of instability in interpersonal relationships, self-image, and affects, coupled with marked impulsivity.

There is no specific cognitive content but others are regarded as dangerous and malignant, and the self is regarded as being powerless and vulnerable as well as being inherently bad and unacceptable both to the self and to others.

6. *Histrionic personality disorder* is a pattern of excessive emotionality and attention seeking.

- 'Unless I entertain or impress people, I am nothing.'
- 'I should be the centre of attention.'
- 'People will pay attention only if I act in extreme ways.'

7. *Narcissistic personality disorder* is a pattern of grandiosity, need for admiration, and lack of empathy.

- 'I don't have to be bound by rules that apply to other people.'
- 'If others don't respect my status they should be punished.'
- 'People have no right to criticize me.'

CLUSTER C – 'ANXIOUS'

8. *Avoidant personality disorder* is a pattern of social inhibition, feelings of inadequacy, and hypersensitivity to negative evaluation.

- 'If people get close to me they will discover the real me and reject me.'
- 'If I think or feel something unpleasant I should try to wipe it out or distract myself.'
- 'Unpleasant feelings will escalate and get out of control.'

9. *Dependent Personality Disorder* is a pattern of submissive and clinging behaviour related to an excessive need to be taken care of.

- 'I am needy and weak.'
- 'I need somebody around available at all times to help me carry out what I need to do in case something bad happens.'
- 'I need others to help me make decisions or tell me what to do.'

10. *Obsessive–compulsive personality disorder* is a pattern of preoccupation with orderliness, perfectionism, and control.

- 'It is important to do a perfect job on everything.'
- 'Details are extremely important.'
- 'I have to depend on myself to see that things get done.'

REFERENCES

American Psychiatric Association (1980) *Diagnostic and Statistical Manual of Mental Disorders*. Washington, DC: American Psychiatric Association.

American Psychiatric Association (1994) *Diagnostic and Statistical Manual of Mental Disorders*, 4th edn. Washington, DC: American Psychiatric Association.

Andrews, G., Crino, R., Hunt, C., Lampe, L. and Page, P. (1994) *The Treatment of Anxiety Disorders: Clinician's Guide and Patient Manuals*. Cambridge: Cambridge University Press.

Antonuccio, D.O., Lewinsohn, P.M. and Steinmetz, J.L. (1982) Identification of therapist differences in a group treatment for depression. *Journal of Consulting and Clinical Psychology* **50**, 433–435.

Barlow, D.H. and Cerny, J.A. (1988) *Psychological Treatment of Panic*. New York: Guilford Press.

Beck, A.T. (1987) Cognitive models of depression. *Journal of Cognitive Psychotherapy, An International Quarterly* **1**(1), 5–37.

Beck, A.T. and Steer, R.A. (1990) *Manual for the Beck Anxiety Inventory*. San Antonio, TX: The Psychological Corporation.

Beck, A.T., Ward, C.H., Mendelson, M., Mock, J. and Erbaugh, J. (1961) An inventory for measuring depression. *Archives of General Psychiatry* **4**, 561–571.

Beck, A.T., Freeman, A. and Associates (1990) *Cognitive Therapy of Personality Disorders*. New York: Guilford Press.

Blake, D.D. *et al.* (1990) A clinician rating scale for assessing current and lifetime PTSD: The CAPS-1. *The Behavior Therapist* **13**, 187–188.

Blanchard, E.B., Hickling, E.J., Vollmer, A.J., Loos, W.R., Buckley, T.C. and Jaccard, J. (1995) Short-term follow-up of post-traumatic stress symptoms in motor vehicle accident victims. *Behavior Research and Therapy* **33**, 369–378.

Brown, G.W and Harris, T.O. (1978) *Social Origins of Depression: A Study of Psychiatric Disorder in Women*. London: Tavistock.

Brown, R.A and Lewinsohn, P.M. (1984) A psychoeducational approach to the treatment of depression: comparison of group, individual and minimal contact procedures. *Journal of Consulting and Clinical Psychology* **52**, 774–783.

Burns, D.D. (1989) *The Feeling Good Handbook*. New York: William Morrow.

Chambless, D., Caputo, G.C., Bright, P. and Gallagher, R. (1984) Assessment of fear in agoraphobics: The Body Sensations Questionnaire and the Agoraphobic Cognitions Questionnaire. *Journal of Consulting and Clinical Psychology* **52**, 1090–1097.

Champion, L.A. and Power, M.J. (1995) Social and cognitive approaches to depression: Towards a new synthesis. *British Journal of Clinical Psychology* **34**, 485–504.

Clark, D.M. and Ehlers, A. (1993) An overview of the cognitive theory and treatment of panic disorder. *Applied and Preventive Psychology* **2**, 131–139.

Coren, S. (1988) Prediction of insomnia from arousability predisposition scores: scale development and cross-validation. *Behavior Research and Therapy* **26**, 415–420.

Covi, L., Roth, D. and Lipman, R.S. (1982) Cognitive group psychotherapy of depression: the close-ended group. *American Journal of Psychotherapy* **36**, 459–469.

Eidelson, R.J. and Epstein, N. (1982) Cognitive and relationship maladjustment: Development of a measure of dysfunctional relationship beliefs. *Journal of Consulting and Clinical Psychology* **50**, 715–720.

Enright, S. (1991) Group treatment for obsessive–compulsive disorder: an evaluation. *Behavioural Psychotherapy* **19**, 183–192.

Evans, M.D. *et al.* (1992) Differential relapse following cognitive therapy and pharmacotherapy for depression. *Archives of General Psychiatry* **49**, 802–808.

Falsetti, S.A., Resnick, H.S., Resick, P.A. and Kilpatrick, D.G. (1993) The modified PTSD symptom scale: a brief self-report measure of posttraumatic stress disorder. *The Behavior Therapist*, **17**, 161–162.

Flemming, B. and Pretzer, J.L. (1990) Cognitive behavioral approaches to personality disorders. In M. Hersen, R.M. Eisler and P.M. Miller (Eds) *Progress in Behavior Modification*. Newbury Park: Sage.

Foa, E.B. and Kozak, M.J. (1986) Emotional processing of fear: exposure to corrective information. *Psychological Bulletin* **99**, 20–35.

Gould, R.A. and Clum, G.A. (1993) A meta-analysis of self-help treatment approaches. *Clinical Psychology Review* **13**, 169–186.

Gould, R.A., Otto, M.W. and Pollack, M.H. (1995) A meta-analysis of treatment outcome for panic disorder. *Clinical Psychology Review* **15**, 819–844.

Greenberg, R.L. (1989) Panic disorder and agoraphobia. In J. Scott, J.M.G. Williams and A.T. Beck (Eds) *Cognitive Therapy in Clinical Practice: An Illustrative Casebook*. London: Routledge.

Haaga, D.A.F., Dyck, M.J. and Ernst, D. (1991) Empirical status of cognitive theory of depression. *Psychological Bulletin* **110**, 215–236.

Hammarberg, M. (1992) PENN inventory for post-traumatic stress disorder: psychometric properties. *Psychological Assessment: A Journal of Consulting and Clinical Psychology* **4**, 67–76.

Hand, I., Lamontagne, Y. and Marks, I.M. (1974) Group exposure (flooding) in vivo for agoraphobics. *British Journal of Psychiatry* **124**, 588–602.

Hayes, S.C. (1995) Working with managed care: lessons from the acceptance and commitment therapy training project. *The Behavior Therapist* **10**, 184–186.

Hooley, J.M., Orley, J. and Teasdale, J.D. (1986) Levels of expressed emotion and relapse in depressed patients. *British Journal of Psychiatry* **148**, 642–647.

Horowitz, M.J., Wilner, N. and Alvarez, W. (1979) Impact of event scale: a measure of subjective distress. *Psychosomatic Medicine* **41**, 209–218.

Howard, K.I., Kopta, S.M., Krause, M.S. and Orlinsky, D.E. (1986) The dose–effect relationship in psychotherapy. *American Psychologist* **41**, 159–164.

Kavanagh, D.J. and Wilson, P.H. (1989) Prediction of outcome with group cognitive therapy for depression. *Behaviour Research and Therapy* **4**, 333–343.

Kenardy, J.A., Webster, R.A., Lewin, T.J., Carr, V.J., Hazell, P.L and Carter, G.L. (1996) Stress debriefing and patterns of recovery following a natural disaster. *Journal of Traumatic Stress* **9**, 37–50.

Kessler, R.C., Sonnega, A., Bromet, E., Highes, M. and Nelson, C.B. (1996) Posttraumatic stress disorder in the National Comorbidity Study. *Archives of General Psychiatry* **52**, 1048–1060.

Kingdon, D.G. and Turkington, D. (1994) *Cognitive–Behavioral Therapy of Schizophrenia*. London: Lawrence Erlbaum Associates.

Larsen, D.L., Attkisson, C.C., Hargreaves, W.A and Nguyen, T.D. (1979) Assessment of client/patient satisfaction: development of a general scale. *Evaluation and Program Planning* **2**, 197–207.

Marks, I.M. and Mathews, A.M. (1979) Brief standard self-rating for phobic patients. *Behaviour Research and Therapy* **17**, 263–267.

Mayfield, D., MacLeod, G. and Hall, P. (1974) The CAGE questionnaire: validation of a new alcoholism screening instrument. *American Journal of Psychiatry* **131**, 1121–1123.

Meichenbaum, D. (1985) *Stress Inoculation Training*. New York: Pergamon Press.

Nezu, A.M. (1986) Efficacy of a social problem-solving therapy approach for unipolar depression. *Journal of Consulting and Clinical Psychology* **54**, 196–202.

Nietzel, M.T., Russell, R.L., Hemmings., K.D. and Gretter, M.L. (1987) Clinical significance of psychotherapy for unipolar depression: a meta-analytic approach to social comparison. *Journal of Consulting and Clinical Psychology* **55**, 156–161.

Norwood, R. (1986) *Women Who Love Too Much*. London: Random House.

Ochberg, F.M. (1996) The counting method for ameliorating traumatic memories. *Journal of Traumatic Stress* **9**, 866–873.

O'Leary, K.D. and Beach, S.R.H. (1990) Marital therapy: a viable treatment for depression and marital discord. *American Journal of Psychiatry* **147**, 183–186.

Olmsted, M.P., Davis, R., Rockert, W., Irvine, M.J., Eagle, M. and Garner, D.M. (1991) Efficacy of a brief group psychoeducational intervention for bulimia nervosa. *Behavior Research and Therapy* **29**, 71–83.

Organista, K.C., Munoz, R.F. and Gonzalez, G. (1994) Cognitive–behavioral therapy for depression in low income and minority medical outpatients: description of a program and exploratory analyses. *Cognitive Therapy and Research* **18**, 241–260.

Otto, M.W., Penava, S.J., Pollock, R.A. and Smoller, J.W. (1996) Cognitive–behavioral and pharmacologic perspectives on the treatment of post-traumatic stress disorder'. In M.H. Pollock, M.W. Otto and J.F. Rosenbaum (Eds) *Challenges in Psychiatric Treatment: Pharmacologic and Psychosocial Strategies*. New York: Guilford Press.

Palmer, S. and Dryden, W. (1995) *Counselling for Stress Problems*. London: Sage Publications.

Prochaska, J.O. and DiClemente, C.C. (1982) Transtheoretical therapy: toward a more integrative model of change. *Psychotherapy: Theory, Research and Practice*, **19**, 276–288.

Rathus, J.H., Sanderson, W.C., Miller, A.L. and Wetzler, S. (1995) Impact of personality functioning on cognitive behavioral treatment of panic disorder: A preliminary report. *Journal of Personality Disorder* **9**, 160–168.

Rothbaum, B.O., Foa, E.B., Riggs, D.S., Murdock,T. and Walsh, W. (1992) A prospective examination of post-traumatic stress disorder in rape victims. *Journal of Traumatic Stress* **5**, 455–475.

Rush, A.J., Beck, A.T., Kovacs, M. and Hollon, S.D. (1977) Comparative efficacy of cognitive therapy and pharmacotherapy in the treatment of depressed outpatients. *Cognitive Therapy and Research* **1**, 17–37.

Salkovskis, P.M. (1996) Avoidance behaviour is motivated by threat beliefs: a possible resolution of the cognition–behaviour debate. In P.M. Salkovskis (Ed.) *Trends in Cognitive and Behavioural Therapies*. Chichester: John Wiley & Sons.

Scott, M.J. (1989) *A Cognitive–Behavioral Approach to Client's Problems*. London: Tavistock/Routledge.

Scott, M.J. and Stradling, S.G. (1990) Group cognitive therapy for depression produces clinically significant reliable change in community-based settings. *Behavioural Psychotherapy* **18**, 1–19.

Scott, M.J. and Stradling, S.G. (1992) *Counselling for Post-traumatic Stress Disorder*. London: Sage Publications.

Scott, M.J. and Stradling, S.G. (1994) Post-traumatic stress disorder without the trauma. *British Journal of Clinical Psychology* **33**, 71–74.

Scott, M.J. and Stradling, S.G. (1997) Client compliance with exposure treatments for posttraumatic stress disorder. *Journal of Traumatic Stress* **10**, 521–524.

Scott, M.J., Stradling, S.G. and Dryden, W. (1995a) *Developing Cognitive–Behavioural Counselling*. London: Sage Publications.

Scott, M.J., Stradling, S.G. and Greenfield, T.A. (1995b) The efficacy of brief group cognitive therapy programmes for anxiety and depression and the relevance of a personality disorder diagnosis. *World Congress of Behavioural and Cognitive Therapies*, Copenhagen, Denmark, July 11–15.

Scott, M.J., Stradling, S.G. and Lee, S. (1997) The diagnostic accuracy of three self-report measures of PTSD. 13th International Conference of the International Society for the Study of Traumatic Stress, Montreal, Canada, November, 1997.

Seligman, M.E.P. (1981) A learned helplessness point of view. In L.P. Rehm (Ed.) *Behavior Therapy for Depression*. New York: Academic Press.

Selmi, P.M., Klein, M.H., Greist, J.H., Sorrell, S.P. and Erdman, H.P. (1990) Computer-administered cognitive–behavioral therapy for depression. *American Journal of Psychiatry* **147**, 51–56.

Sharpe, M. *et al.* (1996) Cognitive behaviour therapy for the chronic fatigue syndrome: a randomised controlled trial. *British Medical Journal* **312**, 22–26.

Shea, M.T. (1992) Course of depressive symptoms over follow-up: findings from the National Institute of Mental Health treatment of depression collaborative research program. *Archives of General Psychiatry* **49**, 782–787.

Snaith, R.P. and Zigmond, A.S. (1983) The hospital anxiety and depression scale. *Acta Psychiatrica Scandinavia* **67**, 361–370.

Spielberger, C.D., Gorsuch, R.W. and Lushene, R.E. (1970) *State-Trait Anxiety Inventory*. Palo Alto, Ca: Consulting Psychologists Press.

Spitzer, R.L., Williams, J.B.W., Gibbon, M. and First, M.B. (1990) *Structured Clinical Interview for DSM-III-R*. Washington DC: American Psychiatric Press.

Stradling, S.G. and Thompson, N. (1997) Stress and distress at work: Whose responsibility? *British Psychological Society Annual Conference*, Edinburgh, 2–6 April.

Telch, M.J. *et al.* (1993) Group cognitive–behavioural treatment of panic disorder. *Behavior Research and Therapy* **31**, 279–287.

Trimble, M. (1985) Posttraumatic stress disorder: History of a concept. In C. Figley (Ed.) *Trauma and its Wake*. New York: Brunner Mazel.

Van der Kolk, B.A. (1996) The body keeps the score. Approaches to the psychobiology of posttraumatic stress disorder'. In B.A. van der Kolk, A.C. McFarlane and L. Weisaeth (Eds) *Traumatic Stress*. New York: Guilford Press.

Weissman, A.N. and Beck, A.T. (1978) Development and validation of the dysfunctional attitude scale, *Annual Convention of the American Educational Research Association*, Toronto, Canada.

Weissman, A.N. and Beck, A.T. (1979) Development and validation of the dysfunctional attitude scale, *Annual Convention of the Association for Advancement of Behavior Therapy*, Chicago, IL.

Weston, S. (1989) *Walking Tall*. London: Bloomsbury Publishing.

White, J., Keenan, M. and Brooks, N. (1992) Stress control: a controlled comparative investigation of large group therapy for generalised anxiety disorder. *Behavioural Psychotherapy* **20**, 97–114.

Williams, J.M.G. (1992) *The Psychological Treatment of Depression*, 2nd edition. London: Routledge.

Williams., S.L and Falbo, J. (1996) Cognitive and performance based treatments for panic attacks in people with varying degrees of agoraphobic disability. *Behavior Research and Therapy* **34**, 253–264.

Young, J.E. (1994) *Cognitive Therapy for Personality Disorders: A Schema-Focused Approach*. Florida: Professional Resource Press.

Young, J.E. and Beck, A.T. (1980) *Cognitive Therapy Scale Rating Manual*. Philadelphia: Center for Cognitive Therapy, University of Pennsylvania.

Zettle, R.D., Haflich, J.L. and Reynolds, R.A. (1992) Responsivity to cognitive therapy as a function of treatment format and client personality dimensions. *Journal of Consulting and Clinical Psychology* **48**, 787–797.

INDEX

Index compiled by Sylvia Potter